LOGIC

BOOKS BY GORDON H. CLARK

Readings in Ethics (1940)

Selections from Hellenistic Philosophy (1940)

A History of Philosophy (coauthor, 1941)

A Christian Philosophy of Education
The Works of Gordon Haddon Clark,
Volume 10 (1946, 2000)

A Christian View of Men and Things
The Works of Gordon Haddon Clark,
Volume 1 (1952, 1998)

What Presbyterians Believe (1956)[1]

Thales to Dewey: A History of Philosophy
The Works of Gordon Haddon Clark,
Volume 3 (1957, 2000)

Dewey (1960)[2]

Religion, Reason, and Revelation (1961, 1995)[7]

William James (1963)[2]

Karl Barth's Theological Method (1963, 1997)

The Philosophy of Science and Belief in God (1964, 1996)

What Do Presbyterians Believe? (1965, 1985)

Peter Speaks Today (1967)[3]

The Philosophy of Gordon H. Clark (1968)[4]

Biblical Predestination (1969)[5]

Historiography: Secular and Religious (1971, 1994)

II Peter (1972)[3]

The Johannine Logos (1972, 1989)[8]

Three Types of Religious Philosophy (1973, 1989)[7]

First Corinthians (1975, 1991)

Colossians (1979, 1989)[9]

Predestination in the Old Testament (1979)[5]

I and II Peter (1980)[3]

Language and Theology (1980, 1993)

First John (1980, 1992)

God's Hammer: The Bible and Its Critics (1982, 1995)

Behaviorism and Christianity (1982)

Faith and Saving Faith (1983, 1990)[8]

In Defense of Theology (1994)

The Pastoral Epistles
The Works of Gordon Haddon Clark,
Volume 15 (1984, 1998)

The Biblical Doctrine of Man (1984, 1992)

The Trinity (1985, 1990)

Logic (1985, 1998, 2000, 2004)

Ephesians (1985)[9]

Clark Speaks from the Grave (1986)

Logical Criticisms of Textual Criticism (1986, 1990)[9]

First & Second Thessalonians (1986)[9]

Predestination (1987)

The Atonement (1987, 1996)

The Incarnation (1988)

Today's Evangelism: Counterfeit or Genuine? (1990)

Essays on Ethics and Politics (1992)

Sanctification (1992)

New Heavens, New Earth (First and Second Peter) (1980, 1993)

The Holy Spirit (1993)

An Introduction to Christian Philosophy (1993)[7]

Lord God of Truth & Concerning the Teacher (1994)

William James and John Dewey (1995)

God and Evil (1996)[6]

Philippians (1996)

Ancient Philosophy (1997)

What Is Saving Faith? (2004)

Christian Philosophy (2004)
The Works of Gordon Haddon Clark,
Volume 4

Commentaries on Paul's Letters (2004)
The Works of Gordon Haddon Clark,
Volume 12

---

1. Revised as What Do Presbyterians Believe? (1965)
2. Combined as William James and John Dewey (1995)
3. Combined as I & II Peter (1980) and revised as New Heavens, New Earth (1993)
4. Part One appeared as An Introduction to Christian Philosophy (1993)
5. Combined as Predestination (1987)
6. Chapter 5 of Religion, Reason and Revelation
7. Combined as Christian Philosophy (2004)
8. Combined as What Is Saving Faith? (2004)
9. Combined as Commentaries on Paul's Letters (2004)

LOGIC

GORDON H. CLARK

THE TRINITY FOUNDATION

Published by
The Trinity Foundation
Unicoi, Tennessee 37692

ISBN 0-940931-71-0

CONTENTS

TO THE STUDENT: WHY STUDY LOGIC?

If you are thinking of reading this book or taking a course in logic, then you need reasons for doing so. Why study logic? What can logic teach us that chemistry or history, for example, cannot? Can logic teach us anything, or is life deeper than logic? If you intend to study logic only because your course of study demands it, then another question immediately arises: Why does the curriculum include a course in logic? Why would anyone think logic is important enough to make it a required course?

These are questions that deserve an answer, but the answer may not be exactly what you might expect. Because many people disdain logic, it will be necessary to understand the relationship between logic and morality, for example. After all, many people think one should not study logic. "Life is deeper than logic," we are told. "Life is green, but logic is gray and lifeless." The poets tell us that "we murder to dissect." Many believe that one's time would be better spent in prayer, protesting, or preaching. Or if they are naturalistically minded, they might suggest contemplating one's navel, or the sunset, or performing experiments in laboratories. So why study logic? Perhaps if we understood what logic is, we could better answer the question.

What Is Logic?

In elementary school you studied such things as reading, writing, and arithmetic. These subjects are correctly regarded as basic to all further education: One cannot study history, botany, or computers without being able to read. Reading, writing, and arithmetic are the basics, the tools that permit one to study further, and also to drive, to shop, and to get a job.

But could there be something even more basic than the three basics? Something so obvious that most people do not see it, let alone study it? What is there in common between calculating, reading, and writing? The answer, of course, is thought. One must think in order to read and write. Thinking, just as everything else, is supposed to follow certain rules, if we are to think correctly. Sometimes we make mistakes in thinking. We jump to conclusions; we make unwarranted assumptions; we generalize. There is a subject that catalogues these mistakes, points them out so that we can recognize them in the future, and then explains the rules for avoiding mistakes. That subject is logic.

The Place of Logic

Logic is not psychology. It does not describe what people think about or how they usually reach conclusions; it describes how they ought to think if they wish to reason correctly. It is more like arithmetic than history, for it explains the rules one must follow in order to reach correct conclusions, just as arithmetic explains the rules one must follow to arrive at correct answers.

Logic concerns all thought; it is fundamental to all disciplines, from agriculture to astronautics. There are not several kinds of logic, one for philosophy and one for religion; but the same rules of thought that apply in politics, for example, apply also in chemistry. Some people have tried to deny that logic applies to all subjects, for they wish to reserve some special field—theology and economics, to name two historical examples—as a sanctuary for illogical arguments. What results is called *polylogism*—many logics—which is really a denial of logic.

But in order to think and to say that there are many different sorts of logic, one must use the rules of the logic there is. Let those who say there is another kind of logic express their views using that other logic. It is as though one were to claim that there are two (or more) sorts of arithmetic—the arithmetic in which 2 plus 2 equals 4, and a second arithmetic in which 2 plus 2 equals 5.* Anyone who disparages or belittles logic must use logic, even in his disparaging and belittling, thus undercutting his own argument. This can, perhaps, be better seen by specifically discussing one of the laws of logic.

The Laws of Logic

The first law of logic is called the law of contradiction, but recently some people have begun to call it the law of non-contradiction: The two phrases refer to the same law. Aristotle expressed the law in these words: "The same attribute cannot at the same time belong and not belong to the same subject and in the same respect." The law is expressed symbolically as: "Not both A and not-A." A maple leaf may indeed be both green and not-green (yellow), but it cannot be both green and yellow at the same time and in the same respect—it is green in the summer, yellow in the fall. If it is green and yellow at the same time, it cannot be green and yellow in the same respect; one part, however small, will be green, another part yellow. Greenness and not-greenness cannot at the same time and in the same way belong to a maple leaf.

---

* Do not be confused by different bases in arithmetic. I am speaking of ideas, not words.

To suggest another example: A line many be both curved and straight, but not in the same respect. One portion of it may be curved, another portion straight, but the same portion cannot be both curved and straight.

The law of contradiction means something more. It means that every word in the sentence "The line is straight" has a specific meaning. The word *the* does not mean *any, all,* or *no.* The word *line* does not mean *dog, dandelion,* or *doughnut.* The word *is* does not mean *is not.* The word *straight* does not mean *white,* or anything else. Each word has a definite meaning. In order to have a definite meaning, a word must not only mean something, it must also *not* mean something. The word *line* means *line,* but it also does *not* mean not-line—*dog, sunrise,* or *Jerusalem,* for example.

If the word *line* were to mean everything, it would mean nothing; and no one, including you, would have the foggiest idea what you mean when you say the word *line.* The law of contradiction means that each word, to have a meaning, must also *not* mean something.

Logic and Morality

What do this law and the rest of logic have to do with morality? Simply this: When the Bible says, "You shall not covet," each word has a specific meaning. Attacking logic means attacking morality. If logic is disdained, then the distinctions between right and wrong, good and evil, just and unjust, merciful and ruthless also disappear. Without logic, God's words, "You shall do no murder," really mean: "You shall murder daily" or "Stalin was Prince of Wales," or any of an infinite number of other things. That means, without logic, words are meaningless. The rejection of logic means the end of morality, for morality and ethics depend on understanding. Without understanding, there can be no morality. One must understand the Ten Commandments before one can obey them. If logic is irrelevant or irreligious, moral behavior is impossible, and the "practical" religion of those who belittle logic cannot be practiced at all.

Something even worse, if anything could be worse, follows from rejecting logic. If logic does not govern all thought and expression, then one cannot tell true from false. If one rejects logic, then when the Bible says that Jesus suffered under Pontius Pilate, was crucified, dead, and buried, and rose again the third day, these words actually mean that Jesus did *not* suffer, was *not* crucified, did *not* die, was *not* buried, and did *not* rise again, as well as that Attila the Hun loved chocolate cake and played golf. The distinctions between true and false, right and wrong, all disappear, for there can be no distinctions made apart from using the law of contradiction. Meaning itself disappears.

The rejection of logic became very popular in the twentieth century. It appears that this rejection will continue into the twenty-first century. In matters of morality, one frequently hears that "There are no blacks and whites, only shades of gray." What this means is that there is neither good nor evil; all actions and alternatives are mixtures of good and evil. If one abandons logic, as many people have, then one cannot distinguish good from evil—and everything is permitted. The results of this rejection of logic—mass murder, war, government-caused famine, abortion, child abuse, destruction of families, crime of all sorts—are all around us. The rejection of logic has led—and must lead—to the abandonment of morality.

In matters of knowledge, we are told that truth is relative; that what is "true" for you might not be "true" for me. So 2 plus 2 might be 4 for you and 6.7 for me. If logic is abandoned, then that also follows. Christianity is "true" for some—Buddhism is "true" for others. One result has been a growing antipathy toward Christianity, which claims that all men, not some, are sinners; and that there is only one way to God, through belief in Christ. Absolute truth—

which is really a redundant phrase—has been replaced by relative truth, which is really a contradiction in terms, like the phrase *square circle*. But once logic is gone, truth is also.

The use of logic is not optional. Logic is so fundamental, so basic, that those who attack it must use logic in order to attack logic. They intend the words they write, "Logic is invalid," to have specific meanings. The opponents of logic must use the law of contradiction in order to denounce it. They must assume its legitimacy in order to declare it illegitimate. They must assume its truth, in order to declare it false. They must present arguments if they wish to persuade us that argumentation is invalid. Wherever they turn, they are boxed in. They cannot assault the object of their hatred without using it in the assault. They are in the position of the Roman soldier who arrested Christ, but they do not realize, as the soldier did, that their position and action are dependent upon rules that they reject. They must use the rules of logic in order to belittle logic; he had to be healed by Christ before he could proceed with the arrest.

The Bible and Logic

In the first chapter of the Gospel of John, John wrote, "In the beginning was the *Logos*, and the *Logos* was with God, and the *Logos* was God." The Greek word *Logos* is usually translated *Word*, but it is better translated *Wisdom* or *Logic*. Our English word *logic* comes from this Greek word *logos*. John was calling Christ the Wisdom or Logic of God. In verse nine, referring again to Christ, he says that Christ is "the true Light" who lights every man that comes into the world. Christ, the Logic of God, lights every man. Strictly speaking, there is no "mere human logic" as contrasted with a divine logic, as some would have us believe. The Logic of God lights every man; human logic is the image of God. God and man think the same way—not exactly the same thoughts, since man is sinful and God is holy, but both God and man think that 2 plus 2 is 4 and that A cannot be not-A. Both God and Christians think that only the substitutionary death of Christ can merit a sinner's entrance into Heaven. The laws of logic are the way God thinks. He makes no mistakes, draws no unwarranted conclusions, constructs no invalid arguments. We do, and that is one of the reasons why we are commanded by the Apostle Paul to bring all our thoughts into captivity to Christ. We ought to think as Christ does—logically.

Why Study Logic?

To return to our first question, Why study logic? Our first answer must be that we are commanded to by Scripture. Without learning how to think properly, we shall misunderstand Scripture. Peter warns against those who twist the Scriptures to their own destruction. A study of logic will help us avoid twisting the Scriptures and trying to make them imply something they do not imply. The Westminster Confession, written in England in the 1640's, says that all things necessary for our faith and life are either expressly set down in Scripture or may be deduced by good and necessary consequence from Scripture. It is only through a study of logic that we can distinguish a "good and necessary" deduction from an invalid deduction.

Logic is indispensable not only in reading the Bible, but also in reading history, botany, or computer programs. It is applicable to all thought, and mistaken arguments may be found in every subject. The study of logic will help us understand all other subjects better, not just theology. Therefore, as God said through the prophet Isaiah, Come, let us reason together.

John Robbins

CHAPTER 1
THE DEFINITION OF LOGIC

Have you ever gotten into an argument? Many people use the word *argument* when they mean *altercation*. An altercation is a brawl. An argument is a series of reasons which one uses to prove the truth of what one wishes to assert.

Suppose you want to convince your parents that you must go into town today to buy a pair of gloves. They ask why. You reply: My old gloves are worn out; this is the only day I have off until next week; and the only place I can buy gloves is in town. These are reasons; they aim to prove the truth of your assertion that you must go into town today. In ordinary situations these are good reasons. But they do not quite prove your conclusion. If one of the reasons happens to be false, the argument fails. But even if they are all true, they do not prove the conclusion to be true. For example, you may have no money. Or, if you have some money, there may be something else you need more than gloves.

Now, logic is the study of the methods by which the conclusion is proved beyond all doubt. Given the truth of the premises the conclusion must be true. In technical language, **logic is the science of necessary inference.** From such and such premises the conclusion necessarily follows.

The preceding paragraph with its definition does not quite explain what a necessary inference is. It certainly does not indicate how anybody can detect one. The "how" is what the whole of this textbook is all about. As one professor of philosophy told his college class, "You cannot understand the first chapter of this book until after you have understood its last chapter." So we must proceed in small easy steps.

Most ordinary matters of everyday life, such as buying a pair of gloves, do not need the very strict proof envisaged in the phrase, "necessary inference." You have given some reasons, some good reasons if true; but your parents might reply, "Well, you don't have to buy gloves today; however, it is a good idea, so run along." But contrary to the conditions of family life, necessary inference is indispensable in mathematics. In physics and chemistry it is at least an ideal which must be constantly approximated. And in courts of law the standards of argument are much stricter than at home.

Any college course in mathematics is a good example, but the best example of strict logic in high school is geometry. From certain premises, called axioms, the theorems are deduced necessarily. Given the axioms, the theorems cannot possibly be otherwise. At this point the student will do well to review some of the early theorems; let him observe that they follow necessarily; there is no way to avoid the conclusion. Try this one: In an isosceles triangle the angles opposite the equal sides are equal. Study the proof and just try to squirm out of it!

Mathematics is not the only subject in which necessary inference is necessary. Though many people would not at first think of it, theology must use valid arguments. In fact, if a knowledge of God has any importance at all, we are under great obligation to argue validly. If cancer research requires extreme care, all the more is extreme care needed in Bible study. To be sure, most people believe that it is more important to escape cancer than to escape Hell; but the logic by which they have come to entertain this opinion is poor logic. They need to examine their inferences.

Now, for an exercise, the student should look through

the Bible to see what arguments he can find. Romans 4:1, 2 are an example. The passage is a somewhat complicated argument, and the student may not yet be able to analyze it correctly. For one thing, like the argument for buying gloves, one or more of the premises is omitted. The glove argument took for granted that the student had enough money. It was known to parents and to the student, and did not need to be mentioned. So, too, Paul's argument in Romans 4:1, 2. Something is omitted. Such an argument, one in which a part is omitted or taken for granted, is called an **enthymeme**. Most arguments in ordinary life are enthymemes.

For further practice, the student may look up five instances where the apostle Paul uses the conjunctions *for, because, on that account, therefore,* and try to find the omitted premises, if any. This exercise may well be too difficult for the student at this early stage in the course, for the arguments in the Bible are often quite complicated. But if he can finish the assignment after he has gone three-fourths of the way through this book, it will register his increasing skill. At any rate, selecting such verses will do no harm. Here are a few. The first is a bit rhetorical, and that does not make it any easier.

Romans 6:1, 2	What shall we say *then*? Shall we continue in sin that grace may abound? Certainly not! How shall we who died to sin live any longer in it?
Romans 8:1	There is *therefore* now no condemnation to those who are in Christ Jesus.
1 Corinthians 15:19	*If* in this life only we have hope in Christ, we are of all men the most pitiable.

An extreme enthymeme, that is, a very greatly condensed argument, understood though condensed because everyone knew the unexpressed propositions, occurs in Luke 5:21:

"And the scribes and the Pharisees began to reason, saying, 'Who is this that speaks blasphemies? Who can forgive sins but God alone?' " It is not difficult to turn the rhetorical questions into assertions; but can the logic student expand the verse so as to make the argument complete? The Pharisees were perfectly logical; in this instance the argument is valid; there is no fallacy. We allege, however, that their premises were false.

What then were their premises, and what was their conclusion? As is often the case in actual life, the conclusion is stated first: "Who is this that speaks blasphemies?" In proper logical form this means, "Jesus is a blasphemer." Such is the conclusion. Now, what are the premises that imply this conclusion? One of the premises, also a rhetorical question as the Pharisees spoke it, was "Anyone who can really forgive sins is God." This implies that anyone who claims to forgive sins claims to be God. The totally unexpressed premise is, this Jesus is only a man and is not God. Therefore, in claiming to be God, he is a blasphemer.

This expansion of the argument no doubt impresses the student as tortuous. As a matter of fact, the argument must be expanded somewhat further still, if it is to be formally complete. And this fact should convince the student that arguments in ordinary language can be and often are extremely condensed in form.

These and others that the student can find illustrate how the Scriptures use argumentation. To understand the Scriptures, it is necessary to understand the argument. No student should be disappointed by not being able to decipher these arguments right off . He needs to study logic. But eventually if a commentator cannot decipher them, and show clearly why they are valid, he has missed the meaning of the verses.

Many arguments in ordinary life-situations are equally difficult; yet many people think that they can recognize a bad argument, or a good argument, the instant they see it. They claim to have no need to study logic. In this they are too optimistic. Even if a politician cannot fool all of the people all of the time, he can fool all of the people some of the time and some of the people all of the time. That is why politicians use deceptive propaganda. It usually fools a great number of people. Now, in addition to those Scriptural verses and as another test of native ability, consider these examples.

In a university psychology class the professor struck a tuning fork; then he silenced it and struck another. No one in the class perceived any difference between the two tones. The professor struck the second fork again, silenced it and struck a third fork. No one in the class perceived any difference between the two tones. Question: If the professor strikes the first fork again and then the third fork, can one validly infer that no one in the class will perceive the difference?

This example occurred in a modern university. Some logical examples have come down from antiquity. Back in the Middle Ages they used this one: What you bought yesterday, you eat today. You bought raw meat yesterday, so today you eat raw meat. Now everyone is intelligent enough to see that this is a bad argument. But can you tell why it is bad? Of course, you know that the buyer must have cooked the meat before eating it. But precisely what is the point in the argument itself that fails? Or, try this one: All animals have four legs (we assume that this is true); all things with four legs are bad; therefore, some bad things are not animals: bad tables, for example. Does the conclusion follow from the two premises? If not, what *precisely* is the trouble?

This argument, however artificial it is, is a tricky one; but the methods of logic, to be explained in this book, will make the analysis of such arguments as easy as rolling off a log—or to use a less medieval expression—as easy as falling off a skateboard.

Yet let not this encouraging statement be misunderstood. Arguments are not always easily explained. Many arguments are extremely difficult to disentangle. The reason is that many of these difficulties are not really logical. For example, to come under the rules of formal logic, an argument's terms, as they recur, must bear exactly the same meaning. To use a silly, but therefore clear example, if in one premise we talk about a kid, and mean a young goat, then the word *kid* in the conclusion cannot mean a young boy. English words are often ambiguous. Now, no rules of logic will aid us in discovering ambiguities. One must know English. Often an argument will contain no ambiguous term, but will nevertheless contain an ambiguous phrase. For example, though it is not really an argument, analyze the statement, You can't eat your cake and have it, too. Before you shake your head yes to this common adage, remember the dietician who replied, "You can't eat your cake without having it, too."

During one of this century's terrible wars, a slogan was popularized and printed in the newspapers in large letters: SAVE SOAP AND WASTE PAPER. A bit odd, I say, eh what? Although this sort of thing is more a matter of language than of logic, and should really be included in English courses, it has long been customary to put a chapter in the logic textbooks on "Informal Fallacies." The next chapter will warn the student, first, that there are some problems which formal logic alone cannot solve; and, second, that arguments, discussions, propaganda, advertisements, proofs, debates in everyday life are often very tricky. A person must uncover these informal deceptions before he can apply the formal tests of validity.

CHAPTER 2
INFORMAL FALLACIES

Arguments are invalid either because they contain a formal fallacy or because they contain an informal fallacy. Formal fallacies have to do with the form of the argument. The subjects argued about are many. One may discuss politics, religion, or sports. But though the subject matter differs, all arguments can be reduced to a small number of types or forms. What these are will be explained in the next chapter. Here we need only note that the following two examples have the same form: All men are mortal, Socrates is a man; therefore Socrates is mortal; and all dogs are black, Fido is a dog; therefore Fido is black. Note too that in these examples the word *man* in the first has the same meaning in both its occurrences; and the word *dog* likewise. Informal fallacies are not fallacies of form, but mainly of bad English. Only it is often more deceptive than ordinary bad English.

The last chapter, toward its end, mentioned ambiguity. It also noted that there are two kinds of ambiguity. When a single word has two meanings, we call it **equivocation**. When the double meaning attaches to a phrase, we call it **amphibology**. Some textbooks call it *amphiboly*, but this word does not occur in the main columns of the *Merriam Webster Unabridged Dictionary*.

An example of equivocation has already been given. It was the slogan, Save Soap and Waste Paper. The words *save, soap,* and *paper,* each have a single meaning; but the word

7

waste can be either an adjective or a verb. Newspaper headings often are examples of equivocation. In an endeavor to make a title brief, the editor sometimes produces a phrase that the reader must read two or three times before he guesses the right meaning. Here the student is advised to look over the newspapers of the last week or two and find some horrible examples.

Sometimes equivocation is intentional and witty. Benjamin Franklin, at the signing of the Declaration of Independence, is supposed to have said, We must all hang together, or assuredly we shall all hang separately. Another possibly intentional equivocation, but not so witty, is the case of a teen-ager who replied to the first question of the Westminister Shorter Catechism, "What is the chief end of man?" by saying, His head, of course. The word with the two meanings is the word *end*, but it is not so good an example now as it might have been two centuries ago, for today the word *end* does not mean purpose as frequently as it did then. We do indeed speak of an end in view; but more often we use the word in the sense of a dead end street.

In serious matters the equivocation is harder to detect. Theologians and secularists quarrel over revelation and reason. The secularists boast about reason and charge the theologian with irrationality. The theologians, or some of them, boast about revelation and deprecate "mere" human reason and logic. Both are guilty of equivocation. Today when secularists praise reason, they do not mean what Augustine, Descartes and Spinoza meant by *reason*. These three men meant an intellectual ability to argue. The secularists are (almost unanimously in this twentieth century) empiricists, and by *reason* they mean sensory experience. It is not quite clear what theologians mean, for they differ among themselves. Many of them agree with their opponents that sensory experience is trustworthy and that science arises from it. But they also hold that theology is dependent neither on sensation nor on reason. In this they have two types of knowledge, two sources of information, which two they cannot harmonize in a single system. Some of the more extreme, called Neo-orthodox, somewhat clearly identify reason as the ability to argue cogently, and then claim that faith curbs reason and that Christianity must be self-contradictory. The point of this paragraph is to show that it is sometimes difficult to discover where the equivocation lies, that theological arguments are often complicated, and that practice in analysis is a student's great need.

When it is a phrase, rather than a single word, that has two meanings, we call it **amphibology**. An ancient example, found in many modern textbooks, is that of Croesus. Croesus, king of Lydia, wanted to make war on Persia. But with proper caution, he first consulted the oracle at Delphi to learn what the outcome of the war would be. The oracle replied, If Croesus goes to war with Cyrus, he will destroy a mighty empire. Delighted, he went to war, but to his chagrin the empire he destroyed was his own mighty kingdom.

Or, consider this very Biblical argument. One drug addict says to another: Do unto others as you would that others should do unto you; you would like others to give you some heroin; therefore, you ought to give me some heroin.

Even ordinary English grammar sometimes produces amphibology. Suppose a mother says to her young son, I am not going to take you to the zoo because it is Saturday. This may mean that the mother has other duties on Saturdays and therefore they will not go to the zoo. Or it may mean, depending on the previous conversation, My aim is not to pass a pleasant Saturday, but to give you a lesson in zoology, so put on your coat and let's get going.

The misunderstanding about going to the zoo could be avoided by the addition of another word, or by an accentuation. The mother might have said, We are not going to the zoo *just* because it is Saturday. Or with a certain tone of voice she could have said, We are not going to the zoo (slight pause) because it is Saturday. These modifications of speech introduce another type of fallacy, called the fallacy of **accent**.

There is a common saying that we should speak only good of the dead. If this sentence is spoken in a calm, unaccented tone, it has its intended meaning. But suppose one should say, *We* should not speak ill of the dead—(but we shall encourage others to do so). Or, we may accent the second word: We *should* not speak ill—(but we shall do so nonetheless). Or, again, We should not *speak* ill of the dead— (but we are going to publish his misdeed in the newspapers). Or, finally, We should not speak ill of the *dead*— (but I am sure going to blacken his living brother's reputation).

This source of misunderstanding often plagues authors and readers of books. If an author is a good public speaker, he constantly uses inflections of the voice; and his auditors can easily understand. But if he publishes his speeches, a reader, particularly the many readers who have not heard him lecture, miss the inflection and actually suffer from serious misunderstandings. To take a less erudite example from common slang: After one person makes a statement, the other person may reply, Oh yes. But if the *yes* is pronounced with a rising sneer, it means *no*, sarcastically.

The fallacy of accent and the fallacy of equivocation somewhat overlap. In fact, many of the examples in this chapter can as well be classified as one or as the other, or even as one of the fallacies yet to be mentioned. Classification of informal fallacies is not systematic. The classes are not watertight. There are of course fallacies that are definitely not equivocation, but such a one may be equally two or more other types at the same time.

However, let us examine one more fallacy of accent or equivocation. In the celebration of the Lord's Supper, the minister may say, Drink ye all of it. If he accents the word *all*, makes no pause, and slurs the word *of*, the idea is that all the wine must be consumed before the end of the service. None may remain over. But if he pauses after the word *all* and accents the word *of*, it means that everybody present should partake.

Fortunately the Greek language of the New Testament is not so ambiguous as English. There are indeed some ambiguities in Greek, but not so many. In this case the word *all*, by reason of its declensional form, is masculine plural, and not neuter singular. The meaning is clear.

Liberal theologians have often used ambiguity, either equivocation or amphibology, to undermine Biblical doctrines. They substitute a vague word or phrase for one that is univocal. *Univocal* means to have one meaning. For example, we speak of Christ's *sacrifice* on the cross. Well, it was indeed a sacrifice; but it was not a sacrifice in the sense that a bunt in baseball is. Now, a bunt or a sacrifice fly is a sacrifice; indeed it is a substitutionary sacrifice, for the batter is put out instead of the runner on second or third. And Christ's sacrifice was substitutionary. Christ's sacrifice and the pinch hitter's sacrifice overlap in meaning. But they are not identical in meaning. The word *sacrifice* covers many different situations. Christ's sacrifice propitiated the offended Deity. To use ambiguous, general, all inclusive, vague terms, such as *sacrifice*, and remain silent about the expiation of sin and the propitiation of God, dilutes the Gospel message through equivocation. The notion of propitiation, and God's justice, is an idea most distasteful to theological liberals. Hence, when the Bible is translated, the word *propitiation*, in some versions, is replaced by a more general and hence ambiguous phrase. The New International Version does this. It uses the phrase "sacrifice of atonement." But there are many forms of atonement. Propitiation is one; but there are others. For example, people used to speak of a criminal's having paid his debt to society by a year in jail. Such a man may have atoned for his sin, but very likely he did not propitiate his victim. The result of vague or too general phraseology is that the people in the pews, who have not much logical sense, accept the new translation; they may even retain the notion of propitiation; but they may soon forget, and a later generation, which does not remember the older, more accurate translations, never learns the idea of propitiation. Thus the Gospel fades from people's minds.

This should be enough to show the student that logic is not merely a matter of trivial, artificial illustrations. Logic books have their flaws. The examples tend to be trivial or artificial. If historical, and not artificial, they are generally irrelevant. Benjamin Franklin's remark was witty, but not many of us are going to sign a declaration of independence and risk our lives on it. Nevertheless, ambiguity constantly takes place; and a study of historical, fictitious, and even the most banal artificialities alerts a student to similar possibilities in his situation. A textbook cannot predict what difficulties the student will encounter tomorrow, nor how he may be deceived by television propaganda. If the textbook alerts him, it has served its purpose.

The next type of fallacy is called the fallacy of **composition**. The first example is no doubt banal, but it is not artificial; and it is well within most students' experience. Your school, let us suppose, has a basketball team. You wish to defend its reputation, and so to impress a doubter you point out that player A is a very good player, and that player B is excellent, and player C is without equal, and so on for players D and E. Therefore, you tell the doubter, your school has the best team in the conference. This argument is called the fallacy of composition. The logical reason is that the characteristics of components are not necessarily, nor even usually, the characteristics of the compound. The practical reason is that the players may not be friendly toward each other, have no team spirit, and lose more games than they win.

The example can be adjusted to the political arena. But let us put it backwards. You wish to show how stupid your political opponent is. You wish to expose his argument. Depending on your political principles, and which side your opponent has taken, you can use one or the other of these two rebuttals: Every United States Senator is a wise man, as you say, but the United States Senate is the stupidest body on earth; or, It is true that each Senator is of limited intelligence, but when their knowledges are combined, the Senate is well-nigh infallible.

Chemistry provides another example. Chlorine is a poison; and so is sodium, for if you put it on your tongue, it will burn a hole in it. Therefore, if you combine them chemically and get NaCl, sodium chloride, it is twice as powerful a poison and should not be sprinkled on eggs at breakfast. Just remember that the qualities of the components are not necessarily, nor even usually, the qualities of the whole; nor are the qualities of the whole necessarily the qualities of the parts. Perhaps you do not like chemistry. Then beware of sociology, for it is full of wholes.

Most of the examples in logic textbooks are artificial, but they have the advantage of being simple. Even the chemical example, though not artificial, is simple. Examples for students should be simple, at least at the beginning. But be warned that in the affairs of the world, the fallacies are usually complex and not so easily recognized. Here is one from philosophy. One of the theories about the constitution of the universe is that it is composed ultimately of atoms. These are very small, hard, impenetrable bodies. The theory has the name of materialism. Now, a German philosopher, named Leibniz, did not like materialism. He thought it could not explain the workings of the human mind. So he proposed the idea that the ultimate constituents of the created universe are minds, similar in essence to the mind of the Creator. Of course, minds are spirits; they are not material; they have no extension in space. Leibniz called them monads: indivisible thinking realities. Some of Leibniz' opponents then objected that if materialism could not explain minds, all the less could minds explain bodies, for if you add one unextended object to another and to another and so on, the sum of zeroes is still zero, and you do not have an extended body. This objection to Leibniz is fallacious. It is the fallacy of composition, for the characteristic of the components is not usually the characteristic of the compound; or to put it backwards, there are usually characteristics of compounds that are not to be found in the components.

Just one more example. When Bonnie Prince Charlie, the Stuart heir to the English throne, attempted to overthrow George II in 1745 and reimpose Roman Catholicism on England and Scotland, his troops were Scottish Highlanders. It is probably true that any one Highlander was a braver or more vigorous warrior than any one English soldier. The Highlanders indeed won the first battle. But the Prince's army, even if it had been more numerous as well as braver, was no match for the disciplined English troops. In the second engagement the Highlanders were put to rout before the battle had really gotten under way. Each Highlander was a better fighter than any one English soldier; but the English army was a better fighter than the Highland troops. The student may try to think of some Old Testament examples. He might also do well to study chemistry.

Another type of fallacy, or at least another name given to some fallacies, is, in Latin, **petitio principii;** in English, begging the question. Essentially this means that one of the premises from which the conclusion is deduced is the conclusion itself, somewhat disguised in form. Now, it must be noticed that this type of argument is actually valid. The conclusion follows from the premises by strict logic. It has to, for the premise is the conclusion itself, and any proposition implies itself. But as a proof by which to convince anyone else, the argument is useless. One can say, chess is a better recreation than soccer because soccer is not so good a recreation as chess. Well, of course: Since the two statements are equivalent, if one is true, the other is true. But no soccer player would be impressed.

Instances of begging the question are not usually so obvious as this artificial example. Consider Thomas Aquinas' argument for the existence of God. Is it a petitio principii or not? The sainted Thomas writes: "Whatever is moved must be moved by another. If that by which it is moved be itself moved then this also must be moved by another, and that by another again. But this cannot go on to infinity, because then there would be no first mover, and consequently no other mover, seeing that subsequent movers move only inasmuch as they are moved by the first mover. . . . Therefore it is necessary to arrive at the first mover, moved by no other: and this everyone understands to be God."

Once again, the Greek of Aristotle, from whom Aquinas took his argument, avoids an English ambiguity. The word *move* in English can be transitive, meaning to put something else in motion, or intransitive, meaning to be in motion. Aside from the English ambiguity, which does not occur in Greek or Latin, can the student detect a case of begging the question?

There is another type of fallacy usually noted in the textbooks. It is called the **ad hominem** argument. The fallacy consists in appealing to the character, the situation, the beliefs or prejudices of the person to be convinced, instead of using premises that deal with the subject under discussion. For example, someone may be impressed with Aristotle's view of the soul as the form of the organic body. Then his minister says to him, You believe the Bible; it teaches that the soul remains after the body disintegrates in the grave; therefore you should reject Aristotle and deny that soul and body form a unity such as Aristotle describes.

The trouble with this argument is that the person's belief in the Bible does not prove a future life. The needed premise is: The Bible is true. There is, nevertheless, a certain plausibility in the argument, for a belief in the Bible implies a belief in a future life. Anyone who accepts both Aristotle's view of the soul and also accepts Scriptural immortality is confused to the point of self-contradiction.

Another example works two ways. A candidate for Congress argues: You should vote for me; I will help raise the protective tariff; and you know that a protective tariff is good for the country because you are a manufacturer. More often this ad hominem argument comes in reverse: No wonder you think protective tariff is good for the country: You are a manufacturer, aren't you! This may be called **abusive ad hominem**.

There are many types and varieties of informal fallacies. They cannot be neatly categorized. There are no rules that can automatically detect them. They so overlap that a single argument may well be an example of two, three, or four at the same time. One category in the old logic books was **ignoratio elenchi**. This is translated, ignorance of the refutation. One modern book less literally translates it, "irrelevant conclusion." But all fallacies are examples of irrelevant conclusions. And irrelevancies come in all shapes and sizes.

Socrates in his *Apology*, his defense before the Athenian judges against the charge that he was worthy of death, spurns the frequent device of criminals who bring their wives and children to court and pitifully ask, Who will take care of these, if you execute me? Such a plea is not a proof of innocence; and it is therefore called the fallacy of **argumentum ad misericordiam.**

In Shakespeare's *Richard III*, after murdering all the nearer heirs to the throne, Richard makes an appeal **ad populum.** This is not a very good example, for it did not stir up much enthusiasm.

Another fallacy, one which fortunately can usually be distinguished from the others, is the fallacy of **complex question.** It is the well known device of asking, Have you stopped beating your wife yet? Ordinarily the fallacy is not quite so obvious.

Another and quite common fallacy is called **post hoc ergo propter hoc.** The student must always use these Latin phrases because they will make him sound learned. The translation is "After this, therefore because of this." In the late seventies the Internal Revenue Service undertook to harass Christian schools. Previously the State Board of Education in Ohio brought suit against one. In Kentucky and Nebraska parents were sentenced to jail for sending their children to Christian schools; and in another instance the government forcibly took children away from their parents and put them in foster homes. Then the IRS stepped in and tried to revoke the tax exemption of Christian schools, holding them guilty of race discrimination unless they could prove themselves innocent by certain processes impossible to fulfill in some localities. One of the arguments the IRS used was that these schools were organized just after laws against discrimination were enacted. *Post hoc, ergo propter hoc.* One of the defenses used by the Christians was that the schools were organized just after the Supreme Court banned the Bible and prayer. One might add that they were organized after violence, drugs and sex became intolerable in the public schools. A member of the State Board of Education in Atlanta, Georgia, accepted the resignation of a teacher whose reason for giving up his job was that a student threatened to slit his throat with a switchblade knife unless he changed a grade of D to B. In such situations the non-violent students are put in danger too, and parents are well advised to find a better and safer school for their children. Ignoring all this, the IRS laid down the un-American principle, You are guilty unless you can prove yourself innocent; and backed it up with fallacious logic. This type of fallacy can also be called an argument **ad baculum:** Do as I say or I'll beat you up.

There are other names but not always other fallacies; for the categorization is sloppy and overlapping. Therefore, the chapter will conclude with the fallacy of **accident.** This occurs when some accidental, irrelevant factor becomes the essential point of an argument. The example, deliciously outrageous, comes from medieval Germany.

A noble host invited a distinguished guest to dinner. To honor him, the nobleman instructed the cook to serve roast stork. The servant was a very good cook, and he roasted the stork to perfection. In fact, the odor was so delicious that he could not resist cutting off one leg and eating it himself. Then he carefully placed the stork on its side and served the platter at dinner. The nobleman was greatly perturbed when he saw the stork had one leg missing. He tried to retain his composure, ignored the mutilation, and treated his guest with extraordinary politeness. But he vowed inwardly to cover his outrageous cook with confusion. On the morrow, therefore, he led his servant into the castle yard and pointed to a stork standing there at a short distance. Storks have two legs, he said, what did you do with the stork's other leg last night? But look, said the cook, storks have only one leg. (The stork in the yard was standing on one leg, as storks often do.) Not to be outdone, the nobleman clapped his hands; at the noise the stork put down his other leg and flew away. See, he said to the cook, storks have two legs. But, replied the cook, last night you did not clap your hands.

CHAPTER 3
DEFINITION

In the previous chapter the remarks about ambiguity showed the need of definitions. The next chapter will give several definitions necessary for the development of logic. This chapter proposes to study the methods of definition. Once again we must insist, for it stands repetition, that a valid argument cannot contain any term in its conclusion that has not already occurred in the premises. Therefore, when the same words are found in premises and conclusion, it must be determined that they have the same meaning. There must be no equivocation. Pascal, a brilliant mathematician and philosopher of the seventeenth century, to guard against errors of this type, said, Always replace (in your mind at least) the word defined with the definition.

A serious instance of such a need occurs in the New Testament. James 2:14 and 17 contain the word *faith*. Romans 3:28 also contains the word *faith*. Does the word mean the same thing in both instances? Martin Luther and other great theologians have had trouble on this point; and there are difficulties here beyond that of equivocation; so that a layman may be excused if he cannot solve the problem in five minutes.

Aside from the epistle of James, the word *faith* in the ordinary religious or political discussions of the present day is used and misused constantly. One definition of *faith* is "believing what you know isn't so." Some religious authors and many secularists make a sharp contrast between faith and knowledge, while some theologians identify them. Augustine and Anselm made faith the basis of knowledge. More Latin: *Credo ut intelligam*, I believe in order to understand. In entering upon religious discussions, one must be very careful to make sure what the other person means by the word. Even more importantly, you must know what you mean. Otherwise you don't know what you are talking about. So much for the importance of definitions.

A good enough beginning for the problem of definition, but only a beginning, is the distinction between connotative and denotative definitions. In fact we may say that the term *definition* is itself equivocal. Suppose now we wish to define the term *eligible voters* in such and such a locality. This may be done by saying, A person eligible to vote must be an American citizen, above a certain age, a resident of the State for one year (or whatever the State specifies), and a resident of the precinct for sixty days before the election, and registered. This is called **connotative definition**, because it lists the necessary and sufficient qualifications. The qualifications are necessary: That is, if any one of them is lacking, the person is ineligible to vote. The qualifications are also sufficient: No further qualification can be required. There is, however, another way to define *eligible voters*. It is the list of names on the clerk's registration book. This is called a **denotative definition.** A denotative definition explicitly mentions every individual—person, place, or thing—in the class.

There is an interesting relationship between the two types of definition. Suppose we erase from the connotative definition above the requirement of being registered. This reduces the number of qualifications, but increases the number of eligible voters. Or, conversely, if we added names to the original list, names of children or foreigners, we would have to delete some part of the original connotation. One might say, As the connotation increases the

21

denotation decreases, and vice versa.

This is not strictly true, however. The denotation, that is the list of names, can be increased by having more people register, without affecting the connotation. But there is a more important exception. The rule just given applies only to classes containing a finite number of members. If the members are infinite, strange things happen. Ask a boy in a lower grade whether there are as many even numbers as odd numbers. He would no doubt say, yes. Then ask him, Are there as many prime numbers as there are numbers? Ask yourself. You will probably argue that since primes are scarce, only ten between one and twenty, and fewer as we go on, there must be many more numbers than there are prime numbers. All prime numbers are numbers, but not all numbers are prime.

You had better take this example to your mathematics teacher and listen to his explanation that there are as many of the one as of the other. You may come away thinking infinity is equivocal. Be sure to get a definition of infinity, but don't ask for a denotative definition of the number series.

Although denotative definitions are useful, and practically indispensable in polling places, they are not independent of connotative definitions. The register of voters is compiled by a prior investigation to determine which individuals satisfy the connotative criteria. This is relatively easy to do; but there is a Biblical and theological example that is not so easy. Various orthodox theologians have tried to defend the possibility of miracles against pseudo-scientific claims that miracles are impossible. This debate requires a connotative and a denotative definition. The anti-Christian philosopher David Hume defined *miracle* as a violation of a natural law. Then a Christian might reply: The crossing of the Red Sea as the Israelites were escaping from Pharaoh was a miracle, though it was effected by a strong east wind, so that no natural law was violated. Then Hume would reply: That was not a miracle; it was just a coincidence. The questions for the Christian then become, What is a miracle? and What events in the Bible are miraculous? No denotative definition will help. Or, at least, one must give a connotative definition before he can compile a denotative list. Many debates on miracles sink into the bog of confusion because one or both sides have little idea of what a miracle is. If they have never taken a course in logic, they should have read a few Socratic dialogues.

An ancient method used for arriving at definitions is described as a **tree of Porphyry**. Porphyry was an obscure philosopher, a disciple of Plotinus, in the third century of our era. The method itself comes from Plato, who exemplified it in the *Sophist*, one of his dialogues, by defining an angler. It is called a tree because its diagram has a sort of point at the top and the branches get broader further down. So . . .

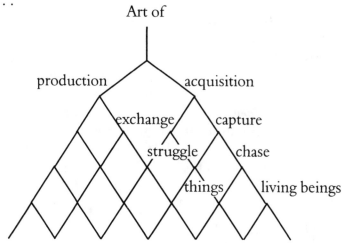

Plato defines angling as an art. Just how art, the top of the tree, is defined, raises more difficulties; but let us proceed.

Angling is an art. Now there are arts of production and arts of acquisition. Of course, an angler does not produce the fish he catches. Acquisition is accomplished either by purchase or by capture. Well, here is the diagram:

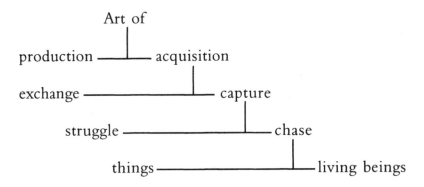

Art of

production ———⊥——— acquisition

exchange ——————⊥—— capture

struggle ————————⊥——chase

things ——————————⊥——living beings

Then living beings are divided into those who have feet and those who float. After arriving at fish, Plato gets to angling by distinguishing between fishing with a spear and fishing with a hook.

Plato was not really interested in fishing. He was interested in defining. After the illustration he more seriously tried to define a *sophist*, and hence the name of the dialogue. Aristotle also used the same method. His terminology was: State the genus, then add the difference; this gives the species. The whole universal tree descends from the supreme genus to the *infimae*, lowest, species. Individuals cannot be defined. This is a quirk in Aristotle because he holds that individuals are the most real of all realities but are nonetheless unknowable. This bit of historical information has the sole purpose of warning every student that surrounding logic is a great deal of philosophy he should take in college and graduate school.

As for trees of Porphyry, one may note that some genera do not conveniently divide in two. The genus *triangle* usually is divided into three: scalene, isoceles, and equilateral. This division is based on the relative lengths of the sides. Of course, one can divide the genus triangle into the species right-angle-triangles and non-right-angle-triangles. And possibly the famous Pythagorean theorem presupposes this classification. To change the examples, botanical species and military ranks are only awkwardly fitted into this dichotomous scheme.

In one sense there can be no debate about a definition. An author may say: This is what I mean by the word ___ . The reader then must take the word in that sense. There is, however, a possibility of debate as to whether the author's definition is close enough to English usage to avoid serious misunderstanding. If he says, by the word *cat* I mean a domestic pet that barks, we are apt to consider him a trifle idiotic, or idiosyncratic. But since ordinary languages use a word in several related meanings, it is not unreasonable for an author to choose one and make it his technical definition. In theology the term *reason* has borne several meanings. It can mean non-revelational knowledge; it can mean knowledge derived by logic alone; and it can mean and has often meant knowledge based on sensory experience. The latter, though it is of frequent usage, seems to veer off a little too far from the etymological meaning of *ratio*.

Sometimes an altercation develops over a "purely verbal" definition. This is a situation where the two definitions have the same intellectual content. For example, one man says, X is a geometrical plane figure so constructed that the enclosed area is greater than any other with an equal perimeter. Another says, No, X is a line every point of which is equidistant from a given point. Both of these expressions refer equally and exclusively to circles. The words are different, but the designated objects are the same.

In twentieth century philosophy another type of definition has become popular, called **ostensive definition**. It is not verbal. It consists of pointing at the object. If someone asks, What is a dog? the other person points to one. Bertrand Russell and especially the Logical (or illogical)

Positivists make this an essential factor in their theories. However, it is hard to point one's finger at the square root of minus one. Or the number three, for that matter. Similarly no one has ever seen a line, or a triangle. And even in the case of visible objects, Augustine's *De Magistro* (*The Teacher*), shows that ostensive definitions are impossible.

Augustine and Bertrand Russell go beyond the limits of an elementary textbook on logic. Here it is enough to point out some of the difficulties. So far as formal logic is concerned, the point is that a term must retain exactly the same meaning throughout the argument.

CHAPTER 4
THE BEGINNING OF FORMAL LOGIC

The arguments in the chapter on Informal Fallacies were all somewhat complicated. If we are now to formulate a method for testing the validity of all arguments, in respect of their logic if not of their English, we must begin with the very simplest **form** of argument. The word *form* indicates that we shall pay no attention to the infinitely different subject matters of arguments, but rather consider their forms alone. Instead of saying, All men are mortal, we shall say, *All a is b*. The letter *a* stands for any subject; and the letter *b* stands for any predicate. *All a is b* is the first form in formal logic.

The reason it is possible to construct rules of validity for all inferences is that the forms of assertion are very limited in number. Take all the declarative sentences in the language, and you will find that there are only four types. The first form is, *All a is b*. It stands for All dogs are canines, All storks have two legs, and All revolutionaries risk hanging.

The second form—they are called categorical forms for no sufficient reason—is, *No a is b*. It stands for No dogs are cats, No Christian is a secularist, and No cooks are perfect. The third form is, *Some a is b*. Some dogs are pets, and so on. The fourth form is, *Some a is not b*. Some dogs are not pets. Every simple declarative sentence can be put into one of these four forms.

Incidentally, most logic books do not talk about declarative sentences. They talk about propositions. There is a difference between propositions and declarative sentences. In English one may say, The kick-off was caught by the fullback; or he may say, The fullback caught the kick-off. These two are two different sentences. The subject and predicate are interchanged, and the voices of the verbs are different. But they mean the same thing. A **proposition** therefore is defined as the meaning of a declarative sentence. Some sentences are not declarative, such as commands in the imperative mood, or exhortations in the well-nigh extinct subjunctive mood. Questions, or interrogative sentences, also are neither true nor false. Only declarative sentences are true or false; and it is this common character that is important for propositions. Of course in English rhetoric there are questions that are intended as propositions. They are called rhetorical questions. They are an embellishment of style. They spruce up a speech. But logically they are propositions. A question that is intended as a question is neither true nor false. It can play no part in an argument.

Let us now return—an exhortation, neither true nor false, but one which it is hoped that the student will follow—to the simplest propositions and the simplest form of arguments. Some additional modifications are necessary to reduce propositions to manageable logical form.

In order that logic be as simple as possible, it does not use the verbs of ordinary conversation. Instead of saying, All the track men run well, logic says, All trackmen are good-runners. Instead of saying, No dogs eat hay, logic says, No dogs are vegetarians. The only verb in logic is the verb *to be*, the copula, *is* or *are*. Premises and conclusions therefore consist of subject-copula-predicate, plus whatever relationship is needed, an *All*, *No*, *Some*, or *Some . . . not*.

Now, for practice sake, the student should try to cast some ordinary English sentences into categorical form. He may have been surprised that declarative sentences have only four forms. Only four forms in all the books in the library!

He also needs practice if he wishes to analyze ordinary arguments. It is easy enough to change English verbs into predicate adjectives, or into somewhat awkward phrases. For example, "children run to school" becomes "All children are runners-to-school." Of course, some children may not run. Without the *all* the English sentence is ambiguous. Does it mean, All children run, or, Some children run? If the latter, the categorical form will be, "Some children are runners-to-school." The awkwardness of the English is no difficulty in analyzing arguments. It sounds stupid, but the sense remains clear. When the English sentence contains dependent clauses, relative pronouns, and prepositional phrases, the categorical translation will be extremely awkward; but with hyphens, or by putting phrases between parentheses to make them look like one word, the sense is clear. For example, All (those who have been born in the United States and are at least thirty-five years old) are (legally qualified to run for the office of president). Perhaps now the value of a simple *All a is b* has become evident.

But there are other difficulties in producing categorical forms out of English sentences besides these awkward expressions. Can the student put this sentence in categorical form? Only good students get A's. Does it mean that all good students get A's? No, for some able students goof off and flunk, or at least get only C. What it means is, All students who get A's are good students. Now, this statement may be false, for some bad students may get an A by mistake or by cheating; but the translation given here is the correct translation. Similarly, "None but the brave deserve the fair" can first be translated into, "Only the brave deserve the fair." Then this becomes, "All those who deserve the fair are brave."

Even logic textbooks make mistakes. One author used the sentence, "An elephant has escaped." The zoo or the circus wanted to give the alarm in good categorical form. The author then translated it, "Some elephants are creatures-that-have-escaped." But this is not really what the zoo keeper meant. He meant, "All Jumbo is an escaped-animal." To be sure, the author was not completely wrong, for it is true, under this condition, that Some (an undetermined number) elephants are escapees. In logic *some* can mean one as well as many or few.

However, when the main idea is certainly one, such as Socrates, the logical form requires All. Socrates was in a class by himself, and so we talk about all that class. We surely do not mean "Some Socrateses."

Other English expressions are harder to manage. For example, business firms for advertising purposes may run a contest in which their employees may not participate. The language is: All except employees may enter. Now, this sentence is not hard to understand, but its use in an argument presents some traps. The trouble is that this apparently simple English sentence is two propositions. It means (1) No employees are eligible; and (2) All non-employees are eligible. Now neither of these two propositions implies the other, for not only may employees be ineligible, but others, non-employees, living in the states where contests are illegal or taxed, may also be ineligible. And also, but not usually, the proposition "All non-employees are eligible" does not of itself imply that employees are barred. Now, what may happen is this. The sentence with the two meanings is taken as a premise, and with some other proposition introduces a conclusion. Then someone who takes the major premise in only one sense may decide that the syllogism is invalid, although it is valid by reason of the premise's other meaning. Or, in the opposite direction, the sentence with two meanings may be taken as a conclusion; in which case someone might consider the argument valid because one meaning (he has missed the other meaning) validly follows. If the premises are both simple categorical propositions, no double meaning conclusion can be validly drawn.

There are other English sentences that cause difficulties. Suppose someone exclaims, either in admiration or disgust, "You always squirm out of an argument." The grammatical subject is You, but it is not the logical subject. Clearly "You" is not squirming out of an argument twenty-four hours a day. And of course the categorical form cannot be "Some You." The word *always* is the logical subject, though not in its literal sense. To get the logical form one must take the *always* to mean "every time you get into an argument." Hence the categorical statement will be, "All times you get into an argument are times when you squirm out of it." A proposition is the meaning of a declarative sentence, and colloquial English must be studied to ascertain what that meaning is. Then we can put it into categorical form.

Students often take great pleasure in figuring out puzzles when they occur as parlor games or as challenges in self-improvement tests in popular periodicals. But when it comes to class work, they are not usually willing to look up additional trouble. Hence here are a few examples to which the student ought to add others; but of course he probably will not. However, can the student state the meaning of the following sentences?

Only freshmen need use the back door.

The poor always ye have with you.

Except the Lord build the house, they labor in vain who build it.

When you understand what these sentences mean, you can easily put them in correct though awkward categorical form. If you cannot put them in categorical form, you do not know what they mean.

Accordingly, all propositions are of the form of All, No,

Some, or Some is not. The simplest inference, then, must be an inference that has one proposition for a premise and one proposition for a conclusion. To be sure, very few inferences in ordinary conversation are so simple; but the student must learn about them because more complicated inferences are built on this simple foundation. The problem therefore is to discover how many such inferences there are, and which of them are valid. Such a set of inferences is called **immediate inference** because there is no middle term. "Middle term" will be defined a little later. At any rate immediate inferences are composed of two propositions with two terms. They cannot have three terms, for clearly it is nonsense to infer that some snakes are poisonous on the ground that some poisons are minerals.

Now, if we wish to test the validity of an inference, we must first know what the term *validity* means. We want no equivocation in logic. Strange as it may seem, it is best, in order to prepare for the accurate definition, to give an inaccurate definition first. So we say, An inference is valid, if the conclusion is true every time the premises are.

This inaccurate definition points in the right direction; but as stated it is pretty bad. For example, it would declare valid the following obviously invalid nonsense: George Washington was our first president; therefore, roses and apple trees belong to the same botanical family. Surely the conclusion is true as often as the premise, for they are both always true. But the one does not imply the other.

There is a second and more surprising reason why the definition is bad. The example just given consists of a true premise, a true conclusion, but a wild inference. But what about false premises? Can they validly imply a true conclusion? A false conclusion? Any conclusion at all? Try this example: All Presidents of the United States have been Roman Catholics. Obviously false. Cardinal Cushing was a Roman Catholic. Obviously true. But not merely obviously true. This true conclusion also follows validly from two false premises. (All Presidents of the United States have been Roman Catholics. Cardinal Cushing was a President of the United States.) How can that be? Can falsity imply truth? It surely can. But although the bad definition can defend itself by saying that the conclusion, being true, is true as many times as the premises—for it need be true only once to be true more times than the false premises— this does not explain how we count the "times" a premise or conclusion is true. A true statement is always true. It is not true three times and false five. Hence the bad definition must be amended. It served only to show that there is some relation between the truth of the conclusion and the truth of the premises.

When, however, we consider the forms of inference, the absurdities vanish. The correct definition will be, An inference is **valid** whenever the *form* of the conclusion is true every time the *forms* of the premises are.

It is now required to show how many times these forms are true. To do so, we must consider in how many ways two terms may be related, whether they be dogs, liberal theologians, or rose bushes. There are five such possibilities. First, all *a* can be *b* and at the same time all *b* can be *a*: that is, *a* and *b* are coextensive, even if different English words are used. Second, all *a* can be *b*, but not all *b* will be *a*. For example, all candy is sweet, but not all things sweet are candy. Third, some of the *a*'s, but not all of them, can be *b*'s, and at the same time some of the *b*'s, but not all of them, can be *a*'s. Some books are interesting, but not all are; for example, logic textbooks. And furthermore, not all interesting things are books. Fourth, all of the *b*'s may be *a*'s, but not all of the *a*'s are *b*'s. Then, fifth, none of the *a*'s are *b*'s. No cat is a dog, and conversely. These five relationships among any two possible terms

33

do not correspond to the four categorical forms in a one to one relationship. But there is a very definite relationship. The following diagrams, invented by the mathematician Euler, will show how many times a form can be true.

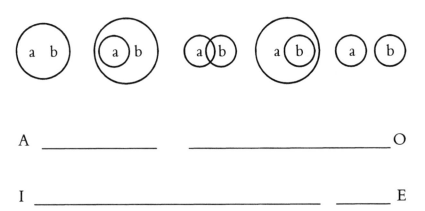

A _____   _____ O

I _____   _____ E

The student will now make an accurate copy of this great work of art, hang it over his bed, and gaze on it in rapture every night. He must note that in two of these five, *All a is b* is true. In only one is *No a is b true*. *Some a is b* is true four times; and *Some a is not b* is true three times. An inference will be valid if the form of the conclusion is true every time the form of premise is.

Underneath the circles four lines have been drawn and labeled A, E, I, O. These letters stand respectively for All, No, Some, and Some is not. A(ab), *All a is b*, is true twice. O(ab), *Some a is not b*, is true three times.

Now, these four capital letters are not just arbitrary letters of the alphabet. They come from the Latin verbs *Affirmo* and *Nego*. The forms A and I are affirmative forms; the forms E and O are negative forms.

We could now start to count the number of possible immediate inferences and test their validity. For example,

I(ab), *Some a is b*, is true every time A(ab) is true. I(ab) is true in the first four diagrams and hence it must be true in the first two. Therefore A(ab) and I(ab) make a valid inference. But though we could now proceed to test all immediate inferences, it may be well to defend the legitimacy of this definition of validity against some opposing views. If this defense becomes too complex, the student may skip the next ten paragraphs.

Many contemporary logicians say that there are four distinct types of validity or implications. They hold that the words *if . . . then* are ambiguous. For example, one logician gives this list:

1. If all men are mortal and Socrates is a man, then Socrates is mortal.
2. If Mr. Black is a bachelor, then Mr. Black is unmarried.
3. If blue litmus paper is placed in acid, then the litmus paper will turn red.
4. If State loses the homecoming game, then I'll eat my hat.

Now, it may be that "if . . . then" has several English uses, and it may be that example four is not an implication at all. But it could be, even so. The argument would be, The loss of a homecoming game is something that disturbs me very much; I am such a peculiar person that when I am greatly disturbed, I eat my hat; therefore, etc. Or it could be understood as a rash prediction, similar in form to one about Hitler and a monkey's uncle, explained later on. The third example can be an enthymeme and when its chemical omissions are made explicit, it will also be a valid implication. In example two, the fact that *bachelor* and *unmarried man* are synonyms does not make the example any less a valid inference. Trivial no doubt, but still valid. Of course example one is standard.

Nevertheless the author of these examples immediately asserts, "Even a casual inspection of these four conditional statements reveals that they are of quite different types." That is the trouble: The inspection has been too casual. This leads him to invent more than one type of implication. He does not say merely that the words "if . . . then" sometimes do not indicate any implication at all; but rather he says "The four conditional statements . . . are different in that each asserts a different type of implication."

Not only so: The author goes on to introduce a fifth type. He says, "Not all conditional statements in English need assert one of the four types of implication previously considered. Material implication constitutes a fifth type," and he proceeds with Hitler and the monkey's uncle. He even gives the correct interpretation of the example. But what he fails to see is that implication and validity are each identical in every argument.

This fifth type most contemporary logicians call "material implication." But then he adds, "In translating conditional statements into our symbolism we treat them all as merely material implications." This is an admission that logic does not need, in fact cannot use, five types. One is enough. Another author, after saying much the same things, concludes, "Briefly, material implication works and works well."

Another logician makes it a little clearer. Examples one and five will suffice. One: If the weather remains warm, we shall have a picnic next Saturday. Five: If anything is a horse, then it is an animal. The first of these, he says, "has an antecedent which implies as a *matter of fact* the particular consequent connected with it. There is nothing in the antecedent itself which necessarily entails the consequent." In proposition five "the consequent is warranted as directly implied in the meaning of the given antecedent. . . . The term 'horse' includes the meaning of 'animal.' "

No doubt this is so; but it furnishes no reason for listing two or four different types of valid implication. The
meaning of the English word *inference* is very broad. It includes the wildest guesses. Many people have inferred that
next winter will be unusually cold because the caterpillars
this autumn are more fuzzy than normal. Though this is a
psychological inference, it is not a valid implication. Even
so, it could be a valid implication if to it were added the
premise "Every time the caterpillars are fuzzy in Septem-
ber, the following winter is rough." So also the picnic on
Saturday. One might say, We have decided to go on a picnic
next Saturday if the weather permits. Therefore, if Saturday is clear and warm, we shall have our picnic. All this
is common English. It is not a great logical discovery of a
new type of validity.

We insist, therefore, that an inference is valid if the form
of the conclusion is true every time the forms of the premises are; and that this definition is sufficient for all logical
purposes.

Perhaps something should be added relative to the sup-
posedly absurd implication: If Hitler is a military genius, I
am a monkey's uncle. This is not really a queer and different type of implication. As an argument it is an enthymeme
and is perfectly valid. Expand the English and it becomes:
If Hitler is a military genius, I am a monkey's uncle; but I
am not a monkey's uncle; therefore, Hitler is not a military
genius. This is a form of the hypothetical syllogism called
modus tollens, later to be explained, and is perfectly valid. Of
course, a person using this type of argument may make false
statements and historical blunders, but logic is not history.
The validity of an argument does not guarantee the truth of
any of its propositions. It is valid if the *form* of the conclusion is true every time the *forms* of the premises are.

Very likely the confusion in these authors is due to the

fact that they are thinking in terms of the incorrect definition of validity, given above. They are thinking in terms of
true and false propositions. All this confusion disappears
when we say, An inference is valid if the *form* of the conclusion is true every time the *forms* of the premises are.

We now return to further study of the forms themselves.
It may surprise the student how much is to be learned about
such a seemingly simple statement as *All a is b*. The next
thing therefore is to ascertain what we mean by saying that
All a is b is an affirmative proposition.

Someone is sure to say that an affirmative proposition is
one that affirms, and a negative proposition is one that ne-
gates. Do you see why that would be useless? Its defect is
that it defines a term by itself. In a definition the term to be
defined must not occur. How then can affirmation be defined without using the word *affirm* or a synonym of it?

It can be done by distinguishing between a distributed
and an undistributed term. A **distributed term** is one
modified by the adjective *all* or *no*. An **undistributed
term** is one that is not so modified. The *all* and the *no* are
often explicitly written out in the proposition; but sometimes they are hidden or implicit. One sees right off that
the subject of the first form, the little *a* after the capital *A*,
is a distributed term. By looking at the second diagram
one will see that no statement is made about *b* as a whole.
It is therefore undistributed. In the first diagram it is possible to make a statement about all *b*: *All b is a*. But for *b* to
be distributed, it must be modified by *all* in every applicable diagram. Hence the subject of A is distributed and
its predicate is not. One will also note that the predicate
of I is undistributed. It is impossible to make a statement
about all *b* that holds in the first four diagrams. Obviously, if the *b* in the second diagram is undistributed, the *b*
cannot be distributed in every one of the first four. Now
then, we have our definition: An **affirmative form** is one

that does not distribute its predicate.

The student can now easily guess that a **negative form** is one that distributes its predicate. But to see this in the diagrams is not so easy. Of course, since *No a is b* means precisely what *No b is a* means—no cats are dogs and no dogs are cats mean the same thing—it is clear that both terms in E are distributed. From *No a is b* it is possible to make a statement about all *b*: All *b*'s are non-dogs.

But the case of O is more difficult. The problem is to make a statement about all *b* that will be true each of the three times that O(ob), *Some a is not b*, is true. If some books are not interesting, can you make a true statement about all interesting things? First look at these two diagrams. The third or last diagram is not needed here, since the previous paragraph took care of it.

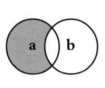 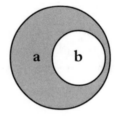

These two diagrams are numbers three and four of Euler's set of five. Here they have been shaded so that the shaded portion is the part of *a* that is not *b*. In the two diagrams there is some *a* that is not *b*. Call this "some a." Then it can be seen that All *b* is non-some *a*. Or more clearly, All *b* is unshaded. Hence it is possible to make a statement about all *b*, from which it follows that O is a negative form. English examples are not frequently encountered because there are few English words to correspond to non-some *a*; but if we put ourselves imaginatively back into the year 1860 we may use this one: Some United States citizens are not northerners means that all Yankees are non-southerners. The diagram would be:

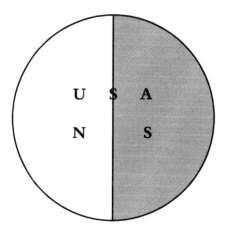

Even if we use the present extent of the United States, and refuse to call Hawaii and Alaska either Yankee or southern, the same result is seen in this slightly more complicated diagram.

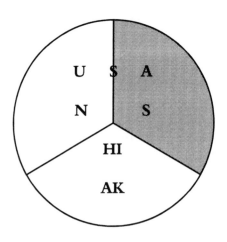

Accordingly, the predicate of O is always distributed, and O is a negative form.

In addition to classifying the categorical forms as affirmative and negative, they must also be given the cross-classification of universal and particular. A and E are universal, because we define a **universal form** as one that distributes its subject. I and O are **particular forms** because they do not distribute their subjects.

The explanation of these terms may seem tedious. But logic begins with what is simple and easy, and builds up to many complexities.

This is mainly a chapter of definitions—definitions by which we become familiar with the characteristics of the simple categorical forms. It is therefore the appropriate place, before we count the number of immediate inferences and determine which of them are valid, to explain three other features of A, E, I, and O. Illustrations can be had from these other things; but eventually it is the forms that interest us most.

Some relationships are reflexive. A **reflexive relationship** is one that holds between one of its objects and that object itself. For example, equality in arithmetic is a reflexive relationship because *two* equals *two*. In logic, implication is a reflexive relationship because any proposition implies itself. The relationship "is less than" is not reflexive because two is not less than two.

A **symmetrical relationship** is one which, if it holds between two of its objects, *a* and *b*, also holds between *b* and *a*. In family affairs *cousin* is a symmetrical relationship, for if John is the cousin of Mary, Mary is the cousin of John. Sonship is not symmetrical because if John is the father of Frederick, Fred is not the father of John. Consider, now: Is "the brother of" symmetrical? If *a* is the brother of *b*, is *b* necessarily the brother of *a*? Good, you figured it out! B may be *a*'s sister. In geometry "is parallel to" and "is perpendicular to" are symmetrical, but in time "is subsequent to" is not symmetrical.

A relationship is **transitive**, if, when it holds between two of its objects, a and b, and also holds between b and c, it holds as well between a and c. If line a is parallel to line b, and line b is parallel to line c, line a is parallel to line c. If moment x is subsequent to moment y, and moment y is subsequent to moment z, then moment x is subsequent to moment z. Now, if John is the first cousin of Mary, and Mary is the first cousin of James, is John the first cousin of James? Or, again, if a is the brother of b, and b is the brother of c, is a necessarily the brother of c? Be careful, now.

Some relationships are none of the three types. Some have two or even all three characteristics.

If, now, the student has completed his genealogical studies, and knows how many grandfathers he and his cousin have, he may now return to formal logic.

The relationship of implication is not symmetrical because if x implies y, that is, if y is true every time x is true, this does not guarantee that x is true every time y is. If, as we shall see, All a is b implies that some a is b, it does not follow that if some books are interesting, all must be. So, implication is not symmetrical. We saw just above that it is reflexive. It is also transitive, for if x implies y, and y implies z, then x implies z. Transitivity becomes very important in the construction of the syllogism.

The relationship "All is," is reflexive because all a is a. It has to be. Obviously. But be careful: The phrase *business is business* does not always mean what it says. It usually means that shady practices are excusable in business. The term *business* in this phrase is equivocal. Lewis Carroll, the author of *Alice in Wonderland,* met a gourmand in one of his poems, who defended his overeating by the assertion that Dinner is Dinner, and Tea is Tea. Lewis Carroll deflated (well, that is perhaps not the most literal term to use) the gourmand by replying:

> Wherefore cease;
> Let thy scant knowlege find increase:
> Say men are men and geese are geese.

The three relationships now explained are not the only ones that are important for the categorical forms. There are four others, and we cannot do without them. The four are **contradiction, contrariety, subalternation,** and **subcontrariety.**

As was said a few paragraphs ago, the student may well be amazed at how complicated a simple form like All *a* is *b*, is.

Here are the definitions, and they have already been pictured by the lines drawn under Euler's diagrams. It is indeed a great work of art.

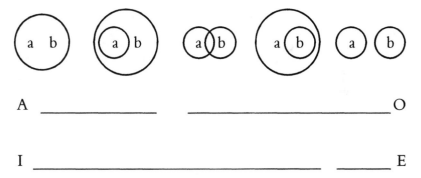

Two forms, or two propositions, are **contradictory** if they cannot both be true and cannot both be false. Since the lines under A and O meet without overlapping, that is, they exhaust all five possibilities, they are contradictories.

Two forms are **contrary** if they cannot both be true but may both be false. The lines under E and A do not overlap, which means that they cannot both be true in any instance; and since they do not exhaust all five possibilities, they may both be false in a given instance. In the instance that some

43

books are interesting, pictured in the third diagram, both A and E are false. They are contraries.

Subalterns are two forms that may both be true and may both be false. A and I are subalterns. E and O are subalterns. You can put your finger on a diagram where both are true; and you can put your finger on a diagram where both are false.

Subcontraries are forms that cannot both be false, but can both be true. O and I are subcontraries, for the two lines both overlap each other and exhaust the five diagrams.

This diagram is called the square of opposition.

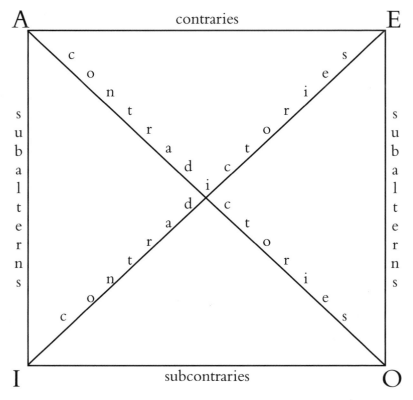

The student should familiarize himself with these relationships by constructing numerous examples. After so doing, he can try to answer the following question. But, watch out, it is tricky.

Suppose the debate team wants to destroy its opponents' argument. To do so, it must prove its own argument. But what should this argument be? Suppose also that so far as the subject matter goes (though this is not always the case) it is just as easy to prove the contradictory of the opponents' position as it is to prove the contrary of the opponents' position. No more research is required in the one case than in the other. Now, the question is, Which of the two, the contradictory or the contrary, most effectively administers defeat?

This chapter has now fairly well exhausted what must be said of each of the four forms singly. At the start, the student could hardly have guessed that so much could be said. People who have never studied logic never guess it. Because they are not aware of and alert to all these possibilities, they make the craziest mistakes in argument. Even when they know concretely that All Yankees are Americans does not prove that All Americans are Yankees, they still make this very blunder in less well known subject matters. You may not believe it, but it is true: In fifty years of college teaching at least once a year, and often once a semester, some college student has committed this blooper. Even a recent theological book contained the assertion: "If a proposition be true, its converse must also be true." Pardon me if I do not give the author's name. He is a friend of mine; but unfortunately he was never a student of mine. I hope that none of the students who look through this book will ever be so irrational.

It is now time to consider categorical forms in combination.

CHAPTER 5
IMMEDIATE INFERENCE

The simplest possible inference is one with a single premise. Syllogisms have two premises; those with just one are called immediate inferences. We must see how many there are, and which of them are valid and which fallacious.

Since immediate inferences have just one premise, and of course one conclusion, the determination of their number is somewhat like the problem of permutations in mathematics. Not exactly, however, for mathematics is more restricted than logic. If you were to give the permutations of two numbers taken two at a time, and the numbers are two and three, the answer would be 2-3 and 3-2. If you list the permutations of four numbers taken two at a time there will be twelve possibilities. Now, since there are four categorical forms, and immediate inference always has two, the problem is somewhat like that of the permutations of four numbers taken two at a time. But with numbers we do not list 2-2 and 3-3. In logic, besides AI, OE, etc., we also list AA, EE, II, and OO—the descending diagonal in the diagram. Hence there are sixteen immediate inferences. The array looks like this:

AA	EA	IA	OA
AE	EE	IE	OE
AI	EI	II	OI
AO	EO	IO	OO

Or, to read these at length: *All a is b* implies *All a is b*. *All a is b* implies *No a is b*. *All a is* b implies *Some a is b*; and to complete the first vertical column, *All a is b* implies *Some a is not b*. When we insert the terms, as usually we must, it is best to write them:

$$A(ab) < A(ab)$$
$$A(ab) < E(ab)$$
$$A(ab) < I(ab)$$
$$A(ab) < O(ab).$$

That little sign between the premise and the conclusion, by which we symbolize implication, is supposed to look like the "is less than" sign in arithmetic. Implication is analogous to "is less than." This is clear from the fact that A(ab) is true twice, and I(ab) is true four times. Two is less than four. But this is only an analogy, for since A(ab) implies A(ab), the conclusion is not always true more times than the premise. Another example is E(ab) implies E(ab). In fact, every form implies itself. Nevertheless, there are several analogies between arithmetic and logic, and the use of the mathematical signs will help to make the similarities more evident. We shall later use the multiplication sign and the plus sign.

Now the question is, how many of these sixteen implications are valid? From what has already been said, the student should be able to point out those which are valid. There are six of them.

The method is very simple. As an example we shall go down the third column. The premise in the third column is I. It is true in Euler diagrams one, two, three, and four, but not five. The conclusion in the first line is A. It is true only in Euler diagrams one and two. Hence it is not true every time that I is true. The inference is invalid. The conclusion in the second line is E. It is true only in the fifth Euler diagram. Therefore it is not true in every one of the first four diagrams. Invalid. The conclusion in the third line is I. It is true in each of the first four diagrams. Valid. Well, of course it has to be, for if a proposition is true, it follows that that proposition is true. It may seem useless to say so, but the system requires it. And if you still think it is useless, just imagine what logic would be like, if it were not so. Then, finally, the conclusion of the last line is O. O is true in diagrams three, four, and five. It is true therefore twice when I is true. But it is not true in diagrams one and two, therefore the inference is invalid.

Let us stop a moment at this last inference. Suppose one of your classmates told you, "Some members of the football team are rotten sports." Would you, a loyal student of dear old Siwash, be inclined to infer that some of the players are not rotten sports? It may be true that some are not; but you cannot validly infer it from the stated premise. Or, to use another example, suppose a secularist in derision sneers, "I have actually found some honest Christians." He expects you to infer that he has found many that are not. In fact, he hopes you will infer that an honest Christian is very rare. Now, it may be that honest Christians are very rare, but under the circumstances you are justified to reply, "Your propaganda ought to find less obvious fallacies." Remember, *some a is b* does not imply that *some a is not b*.

Now that the student has identified the six inferences that are valid, and the ten that are invalid, it may occur to him, if he has been alert, that there are sixteen more possibilities. The reason is that each premise may also have as a conclusion the same forms with their subjects and predicates interchanged. That is to say, the conclusion from A(ab), in column one, line one, might be A(ba). This makes a very different inference. Look at Euler's diagrams again.

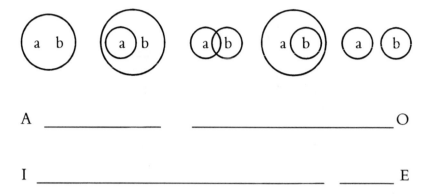

A _____   _____ O

I _____ _____ E

The premise is A(ab), true in diagrams one and two. But now the conclusion is A(ba), true in diagrams one and four. A(ba) is true as many times as A(ab), but it is not true every time A(ab) is. It is not true in both diagram one and diagram two. Thus A(ab) implies A(ba) is an invalid inference. If all Cubans speak Spanish, it does not follow that all who speak Spanish are Cubans. Yet lots of people make this mistake, in examples that are not so obvious.

As an exercise the student should now determine how many of this second group of sixteen are valid, and which they are. To avoid the lengthy phrase "the second group of sixteen" we shall say, the second figure. The definition is, A difference in **figure** is a difference in term order. In immediate inference there are two figures. The only difference possible, when there are only two propositions, is that their subjects and predicates be either in the same order or in reverse order. A(ba) implies A(ba) is just as much first figure as A(ab) implies A(ab). If there should be more than one premise in an argument, there will be more than two figures, as we shall see later on.

But now return to the second figure of immediate inference. There are precisely four that are valid. See in which inferences the conclusion is true every time the premise is. Here is an example. Take the last of the sixteen,

O(ab)<O(ba). O(ab) is true in diagrams three, four and five. Is O(ba) true in these three diagrams? O(ba) is true in diagrams five, three, and two, but not in diagram four. Hence the inference in question is invalid. In English an example would be, Some Spanish-speaking people are not citizens of Cuba, therefore some citizens of Cuba are not Spanish-speaking people. This is invalid, for we take it as factually true that all Cubans can speak Spanish.

There are three ways of identifying valid and invalid inferences. The first is by examples, such as have been given. Because the conditions of an example are so clear and well known, we assume that other examples of the same pattern will be as clear as the example is. Unfortunately this is not always the case. If all triangles are three-sided plane figures, then all three-sided plane figures are triangles. This looks like a valid inference, for both propositions are true. However, it is an accidental example. Sometimes A(ab) is true and A(ba) is true at the same time. But the diagrams show that though this is possible, it is not necessary. The use of examples seems clear and persuasive, but actually it is deceptive as a proof.

The second method of determining validity is the method of diagrams. This looks like a much better method. Nonetheless, it is based on an assumption that may not be true. At least it is an assumption that should itself be demonstrated. The assumption is that the characteristics of circular diagrams are precisely the characteristics of logical forms. Now, there is just a chance that this might be so. Yet, does it not seem strange that circles and forms have precisely the same relationship? Does it not seem suspicious? Suppose you draw a triangle; then you prove that the square on one of its sides is equal to the sum of the squares on the other two sides; will you infer that this is true of every triangle, or will you recognize that what is true of the triangle you happened to draw is not true of some others? Diagrams are useful for some purposes, but that two circles have precisely the same relationships as two logical classes is really suspicious. Later on another method will be explained. Until then we shall continue with Euler's diagrams.

The thirty-two **moods** (individual cases) of immediate inference exhibit some other relationships now to be pointed out. It has already been said that a reflexive relationship is one that holds between an object and itself. Thus the forms A and I are reflexive. But whereas A is not simply convertible, I is. That is to say, I(ab) and I(ba) have precisely the same diagrams and are therefore equivalent. Hence we call I simply convertible. The same is true of E. **Simple conversion** consists of interchanging the subject and the predicate of a proposition. This is a valid process for E and I, but not for A and O.

Two more relationships require first an added complication. In the diagrams there were circles a and b. Obviously everything outside the circle b was *not-b*. Let us symbolize *not-b* with a prime sign, b'. The prime sign will contradict whatever it is attached to, whether a term or a proposition. For example, A(ab') says that all the class a is included in the contradictory of b. E(ab') means that no case of a is found in the contradictory of b. This last example gives us the definition of obversion. **Obversion,** when validly performed, consists in replacing one form with another by contradicting the predicate of the first and changing the quality of the proposition. Thus A(ab) becomes E(ab'). And I(ab) becomes O(ab'). Obversion is indispensable in logic, for it is by this method that the term *No* is defined by the term *All*.

The second relationship is called contraposition. **Contraposition** consists in contradicting both subject and predicate and interchanging them. To contraposit A(ab), one writes A(b'a'). In the case of A, this is legitimate, for if

All Cubans are Spanish-speaking, then clearly All non-Spanish-speaking people are non-Cubans. The student should now discover that contraposition is legitimate for O also, but not for E or I. Consider the diagrams on the following page again.

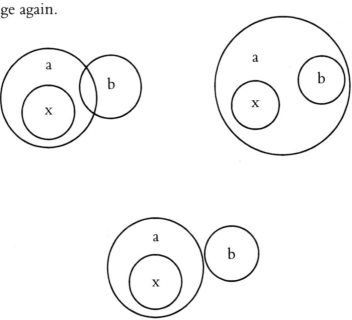

In each one *x* is in *b'*. Therefore, it is true to say Some *b'* is not *a'*.

The diagrams become a little complicated, for now the terms *a, b, a',* and *b'* must all be drawn in. In reducing English arguments to symbolic forms, it is often necessary to use these relationships, for the English argument may contain, say, four terms, that reduce to two because the four consist of two contradictory pairs.

Now try this example: Does the proposition "Some Jews are Israelis" imply the proposition "Some non-Israelis are Gentiles"? Probably half the class will get it wrong; and of those who get the correct answer, two-thirds will give a wrong reason. Well, try again.

Chapter 6
The Syllogism
Diagrams

The next step after immediate inference is the syllogism. Immediate inference had one premise; the syllogism has two. Obviously this is the next step. And it is a most important step because of all the arguments in science, religion, politics, history, and athletics, the greater proportion by far is syllogistic in form.

Some people in each of these fields disparage the syllogism on the ground that it teaches nothing new. The conclusion is already contained in the premises.

Of course the conclusion is contained in the premises; but the way these people make their complaint depends on the equivocal use of the term *contained*. The conclusion is always logically contained (in the valid moods), but it is not always contained psychologically. That is to say, a person by putting together two pieces of information he knows may derive a third proposition he has not previously been aware of.

No doubt you have all heard of people a little too clever who can put two and two together and get five. But many people are not clever enough to put two and two together and get four. Give them two statements and it will take them some time to figure out what, if anything, follows. In detective stories Sherlock Holmes or Perry Mason may get five; but in sober physics the scientist always aims to get precisely four. Remember Galileo and his thirty-two feet per second per second. Syllogisms are not merely useful; they are indispensable.

Galileo knew, from a previous argument, that the velocity of a freely falling body is proportional to the time of the fall. By an easy mathematical deduction—and the mathematics is nothing but a simplified form of syllogistic reasoning—he concluded that a body would fall four times as far in two seconds as in one. He was then able to verify the latter by an experiment and establish the law of freely falling bodies. It is true that a law of physics can never be formulated by logic alone; but it is also true that without syllogistic reasoning no law of physics can be formulated.

The same thing is true when a minister preaches a sermon. Since sermons are not just the reading of a passage of Scripture, but an exposition of a verse or chapter, the minister must—if he will be Scriptural—deduce conclusions based on several verses used as premises. If these deductions are not syllogistic, the sermon cannot be Biblical unless chaotically so and by accident.

At the present time there is a large body of ministers and theologians who reject logic. They are willing to use valid arguments for a few steps, but then they say faith curbs logic. In other words, if several verses in the Bible (supposing them to be true even though these men say much of the Bible is false), if these verses validly imply a conclusion, the conclusion may be false. This view and those who promulgate it are irrational. Validity is the characteristic of an argument by which the conclusion must be true whenever the premises are. These men say, the conclusion must be true, that is, the argument satisfies the laws of logic, but nevertheless it is false. It is true, but it is false. Crazy, isn't it? Well, crazy or insane, in politer language it is called irrational.

The first thing for us to do now is to discover how many "permutations" there are of four items (the forms) taken three at a time. This is surprisingly easy. There were sixteen permutations two at a time. Each of these sixteen may now have A, E, I, O added in succession. Hence there are sixy-four permutations of the categorical forms taken three at a time.

The array would look like this:

	A		A	
AA	E	EA	E	and so on.
	I		I	
	O		O	
	A		A	
AE	E	EE	E	
	I		I	
	O		O	
	A		A	
AI	E	EI	E	
	I		I	
	O		O	
	A		A	
AO	E	EO	E	
	I		I	
	O		O	

We must now figure in the terms. But first a definition should be given. A **syllogism** is an inference with two premises and three terms, the latter so arranged that one term from each premise is also in the conclusion, and one term is in both premises but not in the conclusion: so—

A(ab) A(bc) < A(ac).

Some more definitions are needed. The **major term** is the predicate of the conclusion—here c. The **minor term** is the subject of the conclusion—here *a*. The **middle term** is the one that occurs in both premises, but not in the conclusion. And further, the **major premise** is the one that contains the major term, and, wouldn't you know, the **minor premise** is the one that contains the minor term.

In immediate inference the sixteen permutations became thirty-two inferences because the terms could be arranged in two orders. How many orders, that is, how many figures does the syllogism have? If you go about this in a hit and miss fashion, it will be difficult to come up with the right answer. But the proper method gives the answer, at least the first three quarters of the answer, quite easily. The middle term may be the subject of the major premise and the predicate of the minor—first figure; or the middle term may be the predicate of both premises—second figure; or it may be the subject of both—third figure; or it may be the predicate of the major and subject of the minor. So—

1.	ba	cb	ca
2.	ab	cb	ca
3.	ba	bc	ca
4.	ab	bc	ca

Now we have three terms, and we must figure out how to draw three circles to fit a syllogism. Or, the question may be phrased, how can we draw diagrams that combine the major and minor premises? We want a set of diagrams—three, six, or sixteen—which completely picture the two premises, and then we shall ask, Is the conclusion true every time?

The first of the 256 syllogisms—the student has already multiplied the 64 permutations by four figures to get 256, has he not?—the first syllogism of the array is:

$$A(ba) \; A \, (cb) < A(ca)$$

By convention we write the major premise first; but so far as validity goes, one can put the major second; in fact in English one can state one premise, then the conclusion, and give the other premise last. But by convention, in logic books, we begin by writing the major premise first.

The problem now is to take the two diagrams for A(ba), and somehow include *c* in them. The answer is, impose the first diagram for A(cb) on both diagrams of A(ba); then impose the second diagram of A(cb) on another set for A(ba).

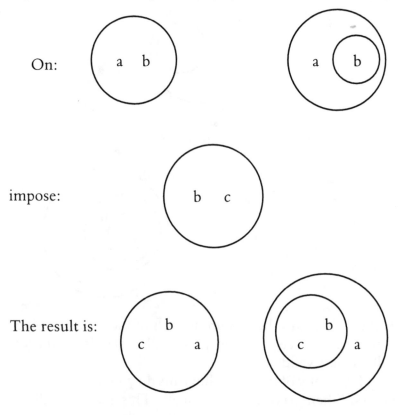

Since *c* and *b* are coextensive in the diagram for the minor premise, *c* and *b* must be made coextensive in both diagrams of A(ba).

Now draw the set for A(ba) again:

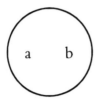 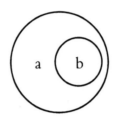

and impose the second diagram of the minor premise:

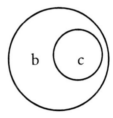

c must be put inside *b*. The result is:

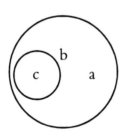 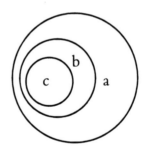

Is the syllogism valid? Examine each of the four combined diagrams and see if in every case All *c* is *a*. It is, and the syllogism is valid.

How many of the 256 syllogisms do you think are valid? Guess. Then make diagrams for all. This is a little tedious, but not quite so exhausting as you might at first suppose. There is, however, a hitch at certain points.

One reason why you do not have to draw 256 sets of diagrams is that a given pair of premises has eight conclusions.

The diagrams above had A(ca) as a conclusion. But E(ca), I(ca), and O(ca) can also be tested with them. Look at the four diagrams and ask, is E(ca) true every time? No. Is I(ca) true every time? Yes. Is O(ca) true every time? No.

But here is a little trick. The diagrams above can also test four syllogisms in the fourth figure. Write A(ba)A(cb) < A(ac). Here c is the major term. Conventionally we write the premises so that the major premise comes first: A(cb)A(ba) < A(ac). So written you see that the middle term is the predicate of the major and the subject of the minor. The premises are the same as those for the first figure, and hence the first set of diagrams will do, but the conclusion is different. Since these same premises can also have as conclusions E(ac), I(ac), and O(ac), we test four other syllogisms with the same diagrams.

Instead of remembering the four figures by SP, PP, SS, PS—that is, the middle term is the subject of the major and predicate of the minor, the predicate of both, the subject of both, and the predicate of the major and subject of the minor—one may use an easier method by drawing a triangle.

First, write the terms, only the terms, in a vertical column.

ba	ab	ba	ab
cb	cb	bc	bc
ca	ca	ca	ca

Now draw lines, one across the top, and another connecting the middle terms.

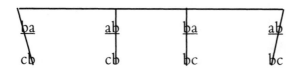

Join these angles and number them:

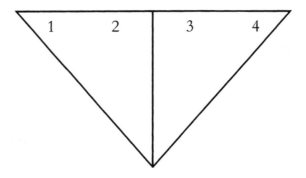

Before going further, make sure that

$$A(ba)\ A(cb) < A(ca)$$
$$A(xy)\ A(zx) < A(zy)$$
$$A(bc)\ A(ab) < A(ac)$$
$$A(ab)\ A(bc) < A(ac)$$

are all the very same identical syllogism.

At the beginning of this section on the four figures, what has since been said was labeled as three-quarters of the correct answer. It is really the complete answer, but because students always ask a certain question, the answer should have another quarter. The question is, Can't we also reverse the terms in the conclusion and get four more figures?

No, we can't. What happens is that the circles in the diagrams are given different letters, but the relationships among the circles remain unchanged. Suppose we take the first figure, A(ba)A(cb) < A(ca), and change it to read A(ba)A(cb) < A(ac). Since the premises of these two syllogisms are the same, the diagrams will be the same.

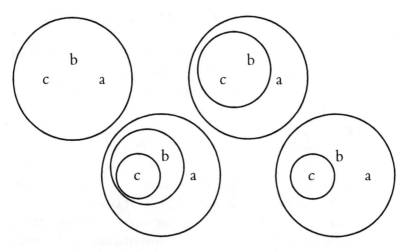

The conclusion of the first of these syllogisms is true in each of the four diagrams; the conclusion of the second is not true in all four. But the present question is, Is the second syllogism a fifth figure beyond the original four? Does changing A(ca) to A(ac) produce a fifth figure?

To find out, we shall draw the diagrams for the ordinary fourth figure, namely, A(ab) A(bc) < A(ca).

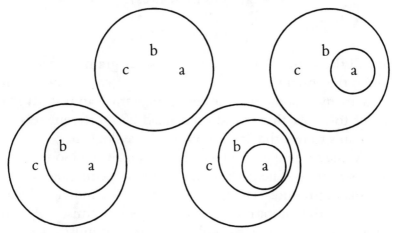

If you look carefully you will discover that each of the three circles in each set of four are in the same relative positions as each of the three in the other set, though they are not in the same order. The only visible difference is that the circles called *a* in the first four are called *c* in the second four. Or in English, the "all cats" which were designated by an *a* at first were in the second case designated by a *c*. There is no fifth figure.

Obviously, so far as validity is concerned, it makes no difference if we label a circle *a* or *x*, *b* or *y*, *c* or *z*, just so long as we do so consistently. Therefore it makes no difference if we label a circle *a* or *b*. If all Athenians are Greeks, we can label the Athenian circle *b* instead of *a*. Of course any other circle symbolizing Athenians in the same syllogism must also be labeled *b*. But we still have one smaller circle completely enclosed by a large one.

It is now time for the student to test every one of the 256 syllogisms. In some cases the same diagrams will do for more than eight moods. Because E and I are simply convertible the diagrams for

$$E(ba) \; I(cb) < E(ca)$$
$$E(ab) \; I(cb) < E(ca)$$
$$E(ab) \; I(bc) < E(ca)$$
$$E(ba) \; I(bc) < E(ca)$$

are all the same. And of course these diagrams also suffice when the conclusion is A(ca), I(ca), or O(ca). Now, count how many moods this one set of diagrams can test. It is a relief to know that you do not need 256 different sets of diagrams to test the 256 moods of the syllogism.

As the student goes on with his testing, he will soon come across a hitch. The general rule is: Draw a complete set for the major premise as many times as there are individual diagrams for the minor premise. If the major premise is A, you must draw two diagrams, and if the minor premise is O, you must draw the two diagrams three times. Then you impose the first O diagram on the first set for A; the second O

diagram on the second A set; and the third on the third. There will be six diagrams composed of three circles each.
   Here is the A set.

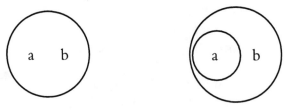

Now impose the first of the O set:

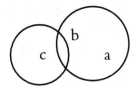

This means that you must overlap a *c* circle on a *b* circle in the A set. But while this is easily done in the first diagram,

it is more complicated the second time. There are three different ways:

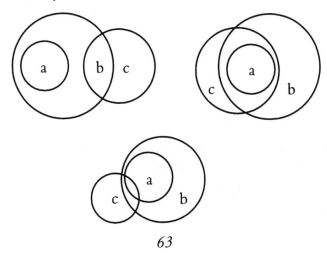

of doing it because the *c* circle, while overlapping *b*, can either take in all of *a*, or only a part of *a*, or none of *a*. Now since validity requires a conclusion to be true in every possibility, these extra possibilities must be drawn in. Hence when you come to test any figure of IO < X, you will have four (I) times three (O), that is, twelve rather complicated drawings.

Actually you will usually not have to draw all twelve simply to test validity. Very likely the third drawing will be one in which the conclusion is false. This is enough to show that the mood is invalid. Yet for practice and understanding it is good to draw all twelve. Worse: Premises II < X require sixteen vicious circles.

Now, if you have all been good little boys and girls and have done your work, I can let you in on a secret. There are 24 valid moods and 232 invalid. You see there are many more ways of arguing incorrectly than correctly. It also happens that each figure has six valid moods: 6 x 4 = 24. They are:

1	2	3	4
AAA	AEE	AAI	AAI
AAI	AEO	AII	AEE
AII	AOO	EAO	AEO
EAE	EAE	EIO	EAO
EAO	EAO	IAI	EIO
EIO	EIO	OAO	IAI

Accordingly, if you get into an argument over politics or breakfast foods, and your opponent uses a syllogism other than one of these twenty-four, tell him he needs a course in logic. Of course, you have to remember the twenty-four.

There are two easy ways to remember: by a poem or by rules. Here is the poem. Beginning with the name of a pretty girl, it will palpitate your heart, unless you yourself are a pretty girl. And besides, all students are enamored with Latin, are they not?

Barbara, Celarent, Darii, Ferioque prioris;
Cesare, Camestres, Festino, Baroko, secundae;
Tertia: Darapti, Disamis, Datisi, Felapton,
Bokardo, Ferison, habet; quarta insuper addit
Bramantip, Camenes, Dimaris, Fesapo, Fresison.

There! That beats anything Virgil or Longfellow ever wrote. It is almost as good as Lewis Carroll's *Jabberwocky.* But it needs some explaining.

With your superb proficiency in Latin you will recognize that *prioris, secundae, tertia,* and *quarta* refer to the four figures. Now, do you observe that each of the names has three vowels? AAA, EAE, AII, EIO, and so on to the end, EIO in the fourth.

It is harder to observe, unless someone points it out, that the initial capitals in figures two, three, and four—B, C, D, F—are all contained in line one. Bramantip relates to Barbara, and Camenes to Celarent. The meaning of this is that if Barbara is valid, so is Bramantip, and if Celarent, so also Camenes. The lower case letters, that is, some of them, show why.

The lower case letters in the first line mean nothing at all, no matter in what line they occur. *S* means simple conversion. If you simply convert the form which precedes the *s* in Cesare, change it from E(ab) to E(ba), you have Celarent. If then Celarent is valid, and if E is simply convertible, it follows that Cesare must be valid.

In Camestres there are two *s*'s. The *t* and *r* mean nothing. The *m* means that after you make the two simple conversions, it is necessary to write the second premise first, in order to put the mood into the conventional form of having the major premise first.

The third and fourth figures have some names containing a *p*. This means conversion per accidens. It was not explained earlier. I and E are simply convertible. A and O are not. But A(ab) implies I(ba); and this sort of looks like a conversion. Even though the categorical form is different, the subject and predicate have been interchanged. This is now called **conversion per accidens.** Hence if you apply the *p* in Felapton, you will get Ferio. Felapton is third figure: E(ba) A(bc) < O(ca). Change the A(bc) to I(bc) and you have first figure Ferio.

Later on you may ask why it is permissible to change an I to an A. Ought it not be the other way around: Change an A to an I? The answer is that the poem works backwards. That is, we do not prove Ferio by Felapton, but Felapton by Ferio. If in any chance syllogism you change a premise from A to I, you cannot be sure of getting a valid mood. But if the mood has an I premise, then when you change it to an A, you are sure to have a valid mood. Hence if Ferio is valid, Felapton must be.

One letter is now left, and it will give you a kick. *K* means **reductio ad impossibile.** The idea is that you start by assuming a given theorem, or syllogism. From this you deduce by valid inference a conclusion you know to be false. This shows that something in your original assumption was wrong. Now take Baroko (second figure)

A(ab) O(cb) < O(ca).

If Baroko is invalid (our assumption) it follows that there must be at least one diagram where O(ca) is false while both premises are true. Or, since the falsity of O(ca) implies the truth of A(ca), there must be at least one diagram where

A(ab) O(cb) and A(ca) are all true. Try to draw such a diagram!

The reason you cannot construct such a diagram is as follows: If A(ab) and A(ca) are both true, then A(cb) must be true, for Barbara is

$$A(ab)\ A(ca) < A(cb).$$

But if A(cb) must be true, O(cb) cannot be true, for they are contradictories. But in our original syllogism, Baroko, O(cb) is true. Now to argue the same thing backwards: If O(cb) is true, A(cb) cannot be true. But we put in A(cb) on the assumption that Baroko was invalid. This led us to contradict our original premise. There is not even one diagram where O(ca) is false. Hence Baroko is valid.

Now, this may have seemed complicated the first time you read it. But read it again. Draw the diagram. And think!

Perhaps this will make it clearer:

Baroko:	A(ab) O(cb) < O(ca)
Assume:	O(ca) is once false.
If so,	A(ca) is once true.
But	A(ab) A(ca) implies A(cb);
And	A(cb) cannot be true.

Because	O(cb) is true.
But if	A(ab) is true as is assumed
Then	A(ca) must be false,
Because	if A(cb) is false, either A(ab) or A(ca) must be false.
Therefore,	O(ca) must always be true.

Now work out Bocardo the same way; and do enough exercises to make sure you have the whole mess firmly in mind.

There is a slight defect in this poem. There are only nineteen names. Yet the diagrams validated twenty-four moods. Perhaps these omissions can be charged up to poetic license. The real reason, however, is that the poet thought anybody would realize that when a conclusion is universal, the corresponding particular is also implied. Hence Barbara stands for AAI as well as for AAA.

Now try these English arguments:

1. Everyone who wears a tuxedo is civilized, and since no zombies wear tuxedos, no zombies are civilized.

2. The study of logic interferes with the pleasures of football, and anything that so interferes should be deleted from the curriculum. Therefore, one of the things that should be abolished is logic.

3. Some animals are not felines, and since all cats are felines, it follows that some animals are cats.

4. Some Greeks are not Athenians, yet all Greeks speak Greek. Therefore, some people who speak Greek are not Athenians.

CHAPTER 7
THE SYLLOGISM
DEDUCTION AND RULES

Drawing diagrams is not the only way of determining validity. Nor is it the best way, for it depends on the suspicious assumption that the properties of circles are precisely the properties of logical classes. Similarly, the theorems of geometry are not proved by the triangles one draws, but by the deductive arguments which they poorly illustrate. Keep in mind that a geometrical line cannot be drawn on a blackboard, for lines have no width and chalk does. To reply that chalk streaks approximate one dimensional lines is an *ignoratio elenchi*; and more obviously the general conic cannot even be approximated.

If now we discard the art work, we must rely on deducing theorems from axioms. Axioms themselves are never deduced because they are the starting points of all deduction. Axioms are assumed. With respect to the syllogism there is more than one way to follow this geometrical method. To make things easy we shall start with immediate inference and then take up the syllogism.

What is needed turns out to be three axioms and two principles of operation. The first principle is: If in any valid mood the antecedent or premise and the conclusion be interchanged and contradicted, the resulting inference is valid.

Axiom 1 is A(ab) < A(ab).
Axiom 2 is A(ab) < I(ab).
Axiom 3 is I(ab) < I(ba).

Applying principle one to these three axioms, we get three theorems:

Theorem 1: O(ab) < O(ab)
Theorem 2: E(ab) < O(ab)
Theorem 3: E(ba) < E(ab).

Obviously, if principle one be applied to these theorems, the axioms appear again. Hence another principle is required to deduce the remaining four moods. The principle itself makes use of two expressions that need to be defined.

Principle two is: In any valid implication, if its premise be strengthened—one could say *blackened* or *pickled*—or its conclusion be weakened—*whitened* or *sweetened*—a valid mood will result.

Blackened, pickled, whitened, and *sweetened* are inserted to show that it makes no difference what English word is used. It is the definition that counts. Some students get confused because they try to understand *strengthened* and *weakened* in the ordinary English sense. But of course, logical forms have neither strong muscles nor weak legs. If we use *pickled* and *sweetened,* the students will no doubt be confused; but at least they will know they are confused, and that is better. But since the terms strengthening and weakening are the customary terms, we shall leave the pickles to wither on the vine.

Hence the definition: The premise of a valid mood is a *strengthened* form of its consequent, and the conclusion is a *weakened* form of its premise.

For example, in Axiom 1, A(ab) is a strengthened form of A(ab); and A(ab) is a weakened form of A(ab). This is of no help. But in Axiom 2, A(ab) is a strengthened form of I(ab), and I(ab) is a weakened form of A(ab). In Axiom 3, note that not only is I(ba) a weakened form of I(ab), but also, since Axiom 3 can be written I(ba) < I(ab), I(ba) is a strengthened form of I(ab). Now we can deduce the remaining four moods.

Theorem 4, A(ab) < I(ba) by weakening the conclusion of Axiom 2; and we weaken it by means of Axiom 3.

Theorem 5, E(ba) < O(ab) by strengthening the antecedent of Theorem 2. The strengthened form of E(ab) is found in Theorem 3.

Theorem 6, I(ab) < I(ab), for Axiom 3 gives us the right to strengthen its own premise or weaken its own conclusion.

Theorem 7, E(ab) < E(ab) is obtained in a similar manner as was I(ab) < I(ab). Or we can also derive Theorem 7 by applying principle one to Theorem 6.

Now, these results are not very startling. The importance of the method is seen more clearly in the deduction of twenty-two syllogisms from two axioms.

For practice the student may deduce the invalid moods of immediate inference. Four axioms will be required and the two principles are slightly different. Principle three is, In any invalid mood, if premise and conclusion be interchanged and contradicted, the result will be an invalid mood. Principle four, watch closely, is, In any invalid mood, if the premise be weakened or the conclusion strengthened, the result will be an invalid mood. Now, the axioms are:

4. A(ab) does not imply A(ba).
5. A(ab) does not imply O(ba).
6. A(ab) does not imply O(ab).
7. E(ab) does not imply I(ab).

From these the student should deduce eighteen invalid moods.

With these exercises completed, the deduction of the syllogism is child's play. The principles are the same—except that since there are now two premises, either one can be used. Use the other one and you get another theorem. From two axioms you must get twenty-two theorems. The axioms are:

Axiom 1:   A(ba) A(cb) < A(ca)
Axiom 2:   E(ba) A(cb) < E(ca).

To get started, notice that Axiom 1, by contradicting and interchanging each premise in succession, gives us

A(ba) O(ca) < O(cb) and
O(ca) A(cb) < O(ba).

What figures are these? And what are their poetical names? In this deduction one must be aware that the theorems do not turn out in conventional form. That is, the terms of the conclusion are not always *ca*; the minor term is not always *b*; and the major premise does not always come first. To determine figure by the triangular diagram one must use the conventional order.

Let us now operate a little on axiom two—Celarent.

E(ba) A(cb) < E(ca).

By contradicting and interchanging the conclusion with the major premise, we get

I(ca) A(cb) < I(ba).

By contradicting and interchanging the minor of Celarent and its conclusion we get

E(ba) I(ca) < O(cb).

Now, by weakening the conclusion of Celarent we get three results because E(ca) implies E(ac), O(ca), and O(ac):

E(ba) A(cb) < E(ac)
E(ba) A(cb) < O(ca)
E(ba) A(cb) < O(ac).

Here we have deduced five theorems from Celarent; but only two of them have *a* as the major term, and two of them do not have *b* as the middle term. Put into conventional form, they look like this:

I(ba) A(bc) < I(ca)
Disamis, third figure.

E(ab) I(cb) < O(ca)
Festino, second figure.

A(ab) E(bc) < E(ca)
Camenes, fourth figure.

E(ba) A(cb) < O(ca)
Celarent weakened, first figure.

A(ab) E(bc) < O(ca)
Camenes weakened, fourth figure.

From I(ca) A(cb) < I(ba), the first theorem deduced from Celarent, by contradicting and interchanging, there come I(ca) E(ba) < O(cb) and E(ba) A(cb) < E(ca). Naturally, after a theorem is obtained, one may deduce further syllogisms from it. The problem now is to deduce twenty-two moods from the two axioms. Be careful: You may and probably will get repeats. You must get twenty-two different moods. Test each one by determining its figure. If you find yourself going around in circles, check with the poem, find out which mood you have missed, and then see what it can be deduced from.

Now, whenever a person is studying an argument on no matter what subject, he may draw some diagrams if he has pencil and paper handy; or he may depend on his memory of the poem; or he may use an easier method now to be explained.

There are five rules, easily remembered, by which the validity of any syllogistic argument may be tested almost instantaneously. These five rules may be taken as axioms, replacing the deductive method given above. Or they may be regarded as a complete induction from the twenty-four moods already proved in some other way. At any rate, here they are:

1. **Two negative premises do not imply a conclusion.**
2. **Two affirmative premises do not imply a negative conclusion.**
3. **An affirmative and negative premise do not imply an affirmative conclusion.**
4. **Two premises in both of which the middle term is undistributed do not imply a conclusion.**
5. **Two premises in which a given term is undistributed do not imply a conclusion in which that term is distributed.**

Many contemporary logicians give six rules. They substitute something different for rule two and preface the whole by saying, "A valid standard form categorical syllogism must contain exactly three terms . . . ," but this is not a rule by which to test the validity of a syllogism. It is a rule, actually a part of a definition, by which to distinguish a syllogism (valid or invalid) from an argument that is not a syllogism at all. When rules for testing syllogistic validity are given, it is presupposed that the arguments tested are syllogisms.

Now the student should want to know whether or not the five rules do the job. To be professional one should make sure that these rules are both necessary and sufficient. The rules are sufficient if their application leaves all twenty-four valid syllogisms untouched, and at the same time shows the invalidity of each of the other two hundred thirty-two. The student may find it tedious to check all two hundred fifty-six; but each check is perfectly easy.

However, there might be a set of ten rules, also sufficient. For example, one such rule might be, two particular premises do not imply a conclusion. But in such a case, there would always be two rules applicable. Try to construct a syllogism to which this rule about particular premises applies, without any others applying. You will find that if you dodge one rule, you get caught by another. This means that while six or ten rules may be sufficient, they are more than sufficient. Some of them are not necessary.

We want therefore to show that each of the five rules is necessary. What does it mean to be necessary? Well, it means you can't do without it. And if you can't do without it, there must be at least one invalid syllogism to which the given rule alone applies. If every time you found that rule one applies, you also found that rule five applies, one or the other would be unnecessary. If the first rule is to be necessary there must be at least one invalid syllogism that does not exemplify either rule two, three, four, or five. Only rule one applies. Such a syllogism is

E(ba) E(cb) < E(ca), or again, E(ba) E(cb) < I(ca).

Let us now see if rule five is necessary. The example cannot have two negative premises, for that would bring in rule

75

one. If it has two affirmative premises, it must have an affirmative conclusion, for otherwise rule two would apply. But if the conclusion is affirmative we have:

A(ba) A(cb) < I(ca) valid.
A(ab) A(cb) < I(ca); rule 4 applies.
A(ab) A(bc) < A(ca); rule 5 alone.

There are other syllogisms to which rule five alone applies. But this one example is itself enough to show that rule five is necessary.

The student should now try to show that rules four and three are necessary. Finally he can test his wits on rule two. Rule two is a slippery character. But it can be done.

These rules are easily memorized and easily applied. If the student forgets everything else he has learned from this textbook, he should at least remember these five rules. For practice he may try to find a syllogism to which rules two and five, but no other, apply; and one to which rules three and four, but no other, apply; and other combinations of rules. Can you find a combination of three rules which together do not apply to any syllogism? It is lots of fun juggling these things around.

This chapter should not end without giving the student some exercises to figure out. The chapter itself was entirely formal; but a preceding chapter pointed out some English difficulties. Now, using English, diagrams, deductions, poetry, and rules, the student must engage in a combat of wits. If you get on a debating team, you cannot expect any consideration from your opponents. The following exercises are less difficult than the debates in real life. The question is: Is the argument valid or not? In either case, show why.

Exercises

1. There must be a performance at the opera tonight, for the outside lights are on, and they are always on when a performance is to be given.

2. The Browns don't eat out when they have house guests. They are eating out tonight, so they must not have house guests.

3. All those who are neither members nor guests of members are excluded. Therefore all Senators are either members or guests of members, for none of those included is a Senator. *(Note: If this looks like an argument with four terms, and so not a syllogism, call to mind that "excluded" and "included" are contradictories.)*

4. The Wrights must have company, for their blinds are down, and they always draw the blinds when they have company.

5. Only seafood is rich in iodine. Game fish is not the only seafood. Therefore not all things rich in iodine are game fish.

6. Not all who were convicted were guilty, for some of the innocent were poor, and the convicted are never rich.

7. A judge sentenced a murderer to be executed at noon on any one of the five succeeding days without the criminal knowing which day until the morning of the day selected. Produce a valid argument to determine on which day the criminal was executed.

CHAPTER 8
HISTORICAL REMARKS

After so much technical and tedious detail the student deserves a coffee break. This will take the form of a brief history of logic.

Since man is the rational creation of the rational God—for not only does Genesis 1:27 say that God created man in his own image, and that after forming Adam's body from earth, God breathed his own spirit into it, so that Adam became a living soul, but 1 Corinthians 11:7 makes it still clearer by saying that *man is the image and glory of God*—since then man is distinguished from the animals by his intellect, it is by his innate nature that he thinks logically. Of course, after the introduction of sin, every man makes mistakes. The so-called noetic effects of Adam's sin consist mainly, or perhaps entirely, of logical blunders. Nevertheless, when a blunder is called to his attention he usually recognizes the mistake. Hence long before anyone tried to systematize logic, men naturally thought logically.

The first deliberate attempt to reduce this type of thinking to systematic form seems to have occurred about the time of Plato. In Plato's dialogue *Protagoras*, Protagoras makes the point, in answer to an objection, that he had said "All the valiant are fearless," whereas Socrates had twisted it as if he had said, "All the fearless are valiant."

Parenthetically, do not be too disturbed at Socrates making a blunder. It was, rather, Protagoras who misunderstood what Socrates was saying. The whole dialogue is very clever. It opens with Protagoras asserting and Socrates denying that virtue can be taught; and it ends by Socrates asserting and Protagoras denying that virtue can be taught. If a student wants practice in analyzing arguments, the *Protagoras* will give him lots to laugh about. But here we are concerned only with the early history of logic.

Let us note first that Protagoras makes a little fuss on this point. He seems proud that he knows it. This would indicate that the principle had only lately been discovered and was therefore a ground for boasting. Then, second, since it is Protagoras, and not Socrates, who makes the point, one may infer that the discovery was not made by the historical Socrates, and surely not by Plato, but, though new, had been disseminated through the educated circles of the day. Plato himself and his disciples, though they advanced geometry to the point of inscribing the regular solids in the sphere, seem to have paid no attention to systematic logic.

Aristotle did; and with such detail that to this day we refer to *Aristotelian* logic. There is indeed another reason, namely, that beginning about 1850 and making great advances in the twentieth century, there is also a non-Aristotelian logic.

Aristotle wrote several short tractates on logic, sometimes more grammar than logic, and added two longer books, the *Prior Analytics* and the *Posterior Analytics*. These, especially the latter, do not diverge downward toward grammar, but rise nobly into the heavenly realm of metaphysics. On the whole, Aristotle's works on logic were not too systematically arranged. The material is somewhat like the early attempts at geometry before Euclid organized the whole thing. Nevertheless these works, translated into Latin, kept alive and stimulated philosophic interest through the Dark Ages and the early Medieval period when not much else was known.

There was one, only one, notable change that the Middle Ages made in Aristotelian logic. Aristotle had a syllogism with three figures; the Middle Ages added a fourth. The reason is somewhat as follows. A middle term, thought Aristotle, had to be either greater in extent than major and minor, lesser in extent than these two, or intermediate between them. He never considered that the middle term or any term could be identical to another. This formal possibility did not fit into his very empirical scheme. Hence for him there are only three possibilities, which we may diagram thus:

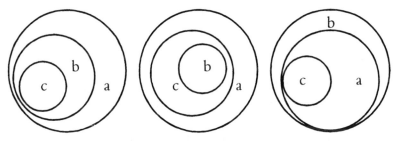

But if instead of this realistic approach, one takes a more formal approach, and considers the possible positions of the middle term, there will be, as we have seen, four figures.

The next development came about the year 1850. Perhaps it was DeMorgan who by his clever *Budget of Paradoxes* stimulated George Boole to construct a symbolic logic. Boole introduced plus and minus signs and made logic look more like mathematics. The minus sign has since been dropped, but zero, one, multiplication, and addition continue. A notable result of this symbolic logic, discovered in the late nineteenth century, enforced by Bertrand Russell in the twentieth, and almost universally accepted today, is the denial of subalternation and the restriction of the syllogism to nineteen, instead of twenty-four valid moods. For example, according to this view, if all Athenians are Greeks, and if all Greeks are Europeans, it does not follow that the

Athenians in the fifth ward—some Athenians—are Europeans. Or, more simply, if all Athenians are Greeks, it does not follow that those in Athens' fifth ward are Greeks.

Although this strange result is all but universally accepted today, the present writer finds a flaw in the modern view. In order to avoid all the ambiguities of ordinary English, and in order to solve some logical puzzles which he did not think otherwise soluble, Bertrand Russell proposed a completely symbolic, artificial language. While his ideal proposal was rejected even by his immediate disciple, Ludwig Wittgenstein, his symbolism for logic has become standard. He reduced the sentence "All Athenians are Greeks," not merely to A(ab), but further to (a<b); that is to say, class *a* is included in class *b*. If this definition be accepted, modern symbolic logic follows without a hitch. Its conclusions follow necessarily. But these conclusions are so restrictive that it is desirable to find a better definition. Russell's implications were necessary, but his definition was not. For example, a better definition of All *a* is *b* is

$$(a < b) \ [(b < a) + (a < b')' \ (b' < a)'].^*$$

Awkward as this formula may seem, it is more in accord with ordinary English than Russell's short definition. Its advantage is that it preserves subalternation. The important question is, Which definition shall we choose? Now, since all important arguments (perhaps with the exception of pure mathematics) are expressed in ordinary English, a systematization of logic should stay as close to English as it can. If a symbolic definition of *All* leads away from serious argumentation, it becomes only a matter of curiosity. Anyone who likes to play games can posit whatever assumption

---

* There is a technical difficulty in this formula in reference to zero. It is similar to the difficulties encountered in the axiomatization of arithmetic.

he pleases and deduce consequences to his heart's content. But he cannot insist that others restrict their serious arguments to his artificial restrictions. In line with this, Russell's short definition, namely, $(a<b)$, though it seems so simple at first sight, proves unsatisfactory in its implications. The longer definition, though cumbersome, does better. Or, perhaps, someone can come up with a less awkward formula that does still better. At any rate, Russell can compel no one to agree with his starting point. This matter of defining a starting point is important.

It is to be noted that there is no logical compulsion to accept one definition rather than another. Russell conjured up his definition out of the free air. The longer formula may have come from cloudy air. But since definitions are not deductions, they can only be judged by their consequences; and the consequences of modern symbolic logic are a restricted sub-system of logic. Aristotelian logic has the nineteen syllogisms that modern logic has, but it also has five more. Surely, if at all possible, it is better to have a less restricted system than merely a sub-set.

Now, regardless of the suggested longer formula, there seems to be good reason for saying that $(a<b)$ does not correctly interpret the English sentence "All a is b." When we say "all *a* is *b*," we mean "every *a* is a *b*." All Athenians are Greeks means every Athenian is a Greek. Now, the *a*'s and *b*'s are variables. They can mean Greeks, rainbows, or typewriters. They can also mean zero or one. One is the class that contains all classes. Zero is the class that contains nothing. Now, since zero is a class, a class used extensively in modern logic, and since one is the class that contains all classes, it follows that $(o<i)$, that is, zero is contained in one. Now try to follow carefully. Since on Russell's view $(a<b)$ defines "All *a* is *b*," then on Russell's view $(o<i)$ means "All zero is one." But it cannot mean this. When we say, in English, that "All dogs are animals," we mean that every dog

is an animal. Hence, if we say with Russell that All zero is one, we would mean that every zero, every class that contains nothing, is a one, a class that contains all classes. Or, to make it still clearer, since zero not only means an empty or null class, but also a false proposition, (o<i) would mean, All false statements are true. Let it be true that zero is included in one: Since zero is a class, and since one is the class that contains all classes, (o<i) must be true. But it is not the definition of *All*. Zero is included in one, but it is false to say, "All zero is one." Hence Russell's definition of *All* is faulty, and his completely valid deductions from this faulty definition have nothing to do with *All, Some,* or subalternation.

Most modern logic textbooks do not analyze Russell's definition. Instead of fixing their attention on the formula as a translation of the English word *all*, they try to explain the peculiar results by a discussion of "existential import." They say that "All *a* is *b*" does not assert the existence of any *a* or *b*; but "Some *a* is *b*" asserts the existence of at least one *a*. Hence, since there is an existential factor in I(ab), and none in A(ab), and since a valid inference cannot have a factor in the conclusion which was absent from the premises, A(ab) < I(ab) must be invalid. But if we insist, these modern logicians must acknowledge that "existential import" is a phrase in ordinary (though not colloquial) English; and that, therefore, whatever force their arguments have must depend on the symbolism. Talk about existential import therefore is irrelevant.

Furthermore, ordinary English, or ordinary logic, has no room for existential import. One of the earlier chapters here said that the forms were called categorical forms for no good reason. The reason, though poor, is that the forms have something to do with predicates or categories. But categorical syllogisms are not "categorical" in the sense of not being hypothetical. So-called categorical syllogisms are indeed hypothetical. Unfortunately the term "hypothetical syllogism" has been used to designate a form of argument somewhat different from the syllogisms of the last chapter. What they are will be explained later on.

However, categorical syllogisms—those of the last chapter—are hypothetical in the sense that the bare logic does not assert the truth of a premise. If we say, "All Athenians are Greeks; therefore, some Athenians, those in the fifth ward, are Greek," and still more obviously if we say, "All snarks are boojums; therefore, some boojums are snarks," the logic as such makes no assertion concerning the existence of Greeks or snarks. That is a matter of history or biology, but not of logic.

To be more exact, instead of saying, "All snarks are boojums; therefore, some are," a logical inference is better expressed as "if all snarks are boojums," etc. But whether snarks live in Athens or Corinth is a question that must be left either to geography or to fairy tales. To repeat for emphasis: This is not a matter that logic alone can decide. Logic alone does not assert the existence or non-existence of anything. It would seem, therefore, that we can dispense with existential import and preserve the validity of subalternation.

Though it is above the usual level of college accomplishment, yet, to prevent these historical remarks from being too brief, we may add that the subject of "Quantification" provides no answer to the previous defense of subalternation.

One author says that there are "types of arguments to which the validity criteria [previously explained in his book and in this one] do not apply." His example is the ancient one:

All humans are mortal.
Socrates is human.
Therefore, Socrates is mortal.

Then the author continues, "Were we to apply to that argument the evaluation methods previously introduced, we would symbolize it as

M
S
∴ H.

"But in this notation it appears to be invalid."

Well, then, this notation must be wrong. Furthermore, this is not a type of argument to which the Aristotelian methods are inapplicable. Since logic alone does not determine the number of objects in a class, the class *a* in A(ab) can be a single object. Socrates is in a class by himself. Therefore

All men are mortal.
All Socrates is a man.
Therefore, Socrates is mortal.

And this is Barbara.

But contemporary logic thinks that singular propositions are something entirely different from universal propositions, and that therefore they cannot be handled by Aristotelian methods. To remedy this alleged defect, the theory of Quantification invents rather complicated formulas. To say the least, this expenditure of ingenuity is unnecessary. When we speak of a class which has only one member, we are speaking about all of that class. Thus a so-called singular proposition is simply an ordinary universal.

CHAPTER 9

OTHER FORMS OF ARGUMENT

If immediate inference has one premise, and the syllogism has two, there are also others that have three or more. They are called **sorites**. As a matter of fact, they are not systematically important, for they are only a string of syllogisms condensed and tacked together. One example of this is A(ab) A(bc) A(cd) A(de) < A(ae).

This breaks down into:

A(ab) A(bc) < A(ac);
A(ac) A(cd) < A(ad);
A(ad) A(de) < A(ae).

Although this sort of thing generates little logical interest, it can be used to write excellent detective stories. First, let us use some illustrations from the author of *Alice in Wonderland*. Lewis Carroll, whose real name was Lutwidge Dodgson, was a mathematician and enjoyed puzzles. He constructed many sorites, leaving their conclusions unexpressed. The reader was supposed to figure them out. Here are some.

Babies are illogical.
Nobody is despised who can manage a crocodile.
Illogical persons are despised.

What is the conclusion? Note that *illogical* is found in premises one and three. Hence they can be connected so as to read:

> All illogical persons are despised.
> All babies are illogical.
> Therefore, all babies are despised.

Note next that *despised* occurs in this conclusion and in the second premise. Thus,

> Nobody is despised who can manage a crocodile.
> All babies are despised.
> Therefore, no baby can manage a crocodile.

The first syllogism is Barbara; and the second is Celarent. Now let us try one with four premises:

1. The only articles of food which my doctor allows me are such that are not very rich.
2. Nothing that agrees with me is unsuitable for supper.
3. Wedding cake is always very rich.
4. My doctor allows me all articles of food that are suitable for supper.

To solve this and others like it, one must discover middle terms that occur in two premises. One must then discover a term that occurs in only one premise, and another term that occurs in only one premise. These latter two will form the conclusion, and the middle terms will link the premises together. The two that occur but once are (1) food that agrees with me, and (2) wedding cake. So we begin.

3. All wedding cake is rich.
1. No permitted food is rich. [Therefore, no wedding cake is permitted.]

4. All permitted food is suitable for supper. [Therefore, no wedding cake is suitable for supper.]
2. All that agrees with me is suitable.
Conclusion: No wedding cake agrees with me.

The first syllogism, with premises one and three, is Cesare. The second syllogism, using the first conclusion as a premise, is Celarent. The third syllogism, by using obversion on the second premise, is Camestres.

With these explanations the student should be able to figure out the next one by himself:

1. All my sons are slim.
2. No child of mine is healthy who takes no exercise.
3. All gluttons, who are children of mine, are fat.
4. No daughter of mine takes any exercise.

Here then is the recipe for a successful detective story. Before you begin to write, construct a sorites, each premise of which is a clue, so that all together, six or eight, necessarily identify the murderer. Mix up the premises into some random order. Then write a chapter on each. Of course you mix in a number of irrelevant details. That is, write a chapter in which premise three is distinctly stated somewhere, and another chapter for clue number five, and so on. Very few of your readers will be able to put them together, and you can make a million out of your best seller.

There are some rules, rather useless rules, for the sorites:

1. **If the conclusion is affirmative, all the premises must be affirmative also.**
2. **If the conclusion is negative, then one and only one premise is negative.**
3. **If the conclusion is universal, all the premises must be, too.**

4. If the conclusion is particular, then not more than one premise can be particular.

The next type of argument is called the **hypothetical syllogism,** namely,

> x implies y
> x is true
> ∴ y is true.

This form is called the constructive hypothetical syllogism, or in our lovely Latin, **modus ponens.** There is also a **modus tollens,** or destructive hypothetical syllogism:

> x implies y
> y is false
> ∴ x is false.

A little consideration will show that there are two corresponding fallacies. First, asserting the consequent; second, denying the antecedent:

> (1) x implies y
> y is true
> ∴ x is true.

> (2) x implies y
> x is false
> ∴ y is false.

No students today remember the return of Prime Minister Neville Chamberlain from his fateful meeting with Adolf Hitler. He was carrying an umbrella, as he usually did. Suppose we now argue:

Chamberlain always carries an umbrella when it rains.
(That is, if it is raining, Chamberlain carries an umbrella.)
Chamberlain is carrying an umbrella. Therefore, it is raining.

Anyone who knew Chamberlain, or who knows London weather, or who knows logic, will know that this is an invalid inference.

Or one may argue,

If the carburetor fails, the engine dies.
The engine has died.
Therefore, I need to rebuild the carburetor.

Even an auto mechanic knows logic when it comes to carburetors. Asserting the consequent is a fallacy.

In religion and politics people often fall into these fallacies, usually because they know and use premises not contained in the argument. Suppose someone quotes Romans 10:9, "If you confess with your mouth the Lord Jesus and believe in your heart that God has raised him from the dead, you will be saved." After quoting this verse the person continues, "the apostle Paul, or John Jones, certainly was saved; therefore he made this confession and believed in the resurrection." In simpler form, Mr. X is saved; therefore, he must have believed this. Our devout friend's argument is fallacious. He has made a logical blunder. What has happened is that our friend is convinced from other parts of the Bible that no one can be saved without believing that God raised Christ from the dead. But this verse, all by itself, does not say so. It says, If you believe, you will be saved. But so far as this verse alone is concerned, it is like the carburetor. If the carburetor fails, the car stops; but from the car's stopping, one cannot conclude that the carburetor is kaput.

A valid argument would be, "Unless you repent, you will all likewise perish." Repentance is a *sine qua non* of salvation. You cannot be saved without repenting. The argument would be, "If you are saved, you have repented." By contradiction and interchange it becomes "If you have not repented, you have not been saved." But even with this verse you cannot validly say, "If you repent, you will be saved." The verse says, Non-repentance results in doom. It does not say, repentance results in non-doom. If this latter be true, some other verses must be used as premises.

To get back to Hitler and, not Chamberlain, but Churchill, consider this:

The Germans may win on land in Russia, France, and Africa, but if the British navy remains intact, they will not be able to dictate the peace. Therefore, if they win both on land and on the sea, they will be able to dictate the peace.

A slightly more complex form of the hypothetical syllogism is the **disjunctive hypothetical syllogism,** namely,

> x + y
> x is false
> ∴ y is true.

This requires an explanation of the plus sign, which symbolizes disjunction. The English word *or* is ambiguous. It has three distinct meanings. In Latin there was a separate word for each meaning, but we have only one.

(1) I hear an animal walking around in the kitchen. It must be either a dog or a cat. Obviously it cannot be both. In Latin this meaning was expressed by the word *aut.*

(2) Its shape was like a sphere or a ball. Here the common word *ball* explains the more technical word *sphere.*

Spinoza, a pantheistic philosopher, used the phrase "God or nature." He meant that the words God and nature should be understood as synonyms. The Latin was *Deus sive natura*.

(3) Suppose you sit next to a man on a plane or bus. He talks about baseball and clearly knows the rules better than you do. You say to yourself, "This man is an umpire or a very devoted baseball fan." Of course he may be both. The Latin word is *vel*.

The problem now is this: Can logic use just one of these three, and yet express the other two when necessary? The answer is that the third sense will serve. In fact some logicians use the letter v to indicate disjunction, as (a v b): *a* or *b* or, of course, both. The letter v is a poor symbol. In the syllogism, when we conjoined two premises, we wrote them A(ba) A(cb). This is multiplication. The letters pq mean that p is true and q is true. Or, *ab* means things that are both apples and brown. Multiplication in logic is conjunction. Similarly, addition in logic is disjunction. The symbol (a + b) means, either *a* or *b*.

There are several cases where logical multiplication and conjunction are analogous; and similarly with logical disjunction and addition. Examples, with their translations beneath them, are

$$a(b + c) = ab + ac$$
a and either *b* or *c* = *ab* are both true or *ac* are both true.

$$ai = a$$
What is both *a* and something, is *a*.

$$ao = o$$
What is both *a* and nothing, is nothing.

a+i = i
What is either *a* or something, is something.

a+o = a
What is either *a* or nothing, is *a*.

To show the relationship between logic and math, therefore, it is better to use the plus sign than the linguistic "*v*", or *vel*.

Now, after some English examples of disjunctive hypothetical syllogisms, we shall return to other more interesting symbolism.

Because of known circumstances you can assert these two premises:

> Florence got a new dress or she went to the party.
> Florence did not go to the party.

From these propositions you may validly infer:

> Florence got a new dress.

But now suppose:

> Florence got a new dress or she went to the party.
> She got a new dress.
> Therefore, she did not go to the party.

If the word *or* had been taken in the Latin sense of *aut*, this would have been valid. But since we have decided to use it in the sense of *vel*, the argument is invalid.

Sometimes the English deceives us. Suppose someone argues:

> Jones is in Texas or he is in Paris.

Jones is in Paris.
Therefore, he is not in Texas.

This sounds valid. If Jones took off from Dallas and flew to France, he could not be in Texas. But the argument does not specify Paris, France. There is also a Paris in northeast Texas, as well as in Kentucky, and some other states.

The rule is: The denial in the minor premise of one of the major's disjuncts implies the truth of the other disjunct. The assertion of one of the disjuncts implies nothing about the other.

Possibly the most interesting of all forms of argument, though not to a symbolic logician, is the dilemma. A **dilemma** is an argument of the form:

$$(x < y) \ (z < w) \ (x + z) < (y + w).$$

These factors can be juggled around some. For example, by contradicting and interchanging the conclusion and the third premise, we get $(x < y) \ (z < w) \ (y + w)' < (x + z)'$.

Analogously to *modus tollens* we have:

$$(x < y) \ (z < w) \ (y' + w') < (x' + z').$$

As usual, the plus sign, indicating disjunction, is not the Latin *sive*, but *vel*. It means either y or w is true, or both. One must be true; both may be. But $(y+w)'$ is different from $(y' + w')$. The first of these says that the disjunction is false; that is, both y and w must be false. The second means that one or the other is false; and while both may be false, both don't have to be false. To construct an English example is slightly difficult, at least difficult enough to show how much clearer symbolism is than English.

First, $(y + w)'$ may mean, It is false that George Washington was a Roman Catholic and Kennedy was a Protestant.

This denial is factually true because Washington was not Catholic and Kennedy was not Protestant; that is, (y'w').

Second, (y' + w') may mean, Either Cleveland is not in Iowa or Kalamazoo is not in Michigan. But it does not mean (y'w') as the above did. It does not mean, Cleveland is not in Iowa and Kalamazoo is not in Michigan, for the first of these is true and the second false. The example means (yw)', namely, It is false that Cleveland is in Iowa and Kalamazoo is in Michigan.

The dilemma is not asserted as an axiom. It can be derived from simpler forms of argument. Here is the derivation: Assume

$$(x < y) < (y' < x').$$

This is a contradiction and interchange. Now multiply both sides by the same factor:

$$(x < y) \ (x' < z) < (y' < x') \ (x' < z).$$

Because of the law of transitivity the conclusion can be condensed to (y' < z):

$$(x < y) \ (x' < z) < (y' < z).$$

Now again multiply both sides by the same factor:

$$(x < y) \ (x' < z) \ (z < w) < (y' < z) \ (z < w).$$

Condensing the conclusion again by transitivity, we have:

$$(x < y) \ (x' < z) \ (x < w) < (y' < w).$$

But $(y' < w) = (y + w)$.
And $(x' < z) = (x + z)$.

So that

$$(x < y) \ (z < w) \ (x + z) < (y + w).$$

Since x, y, z, and w are variables, any English meanings can be substituted, provided of course that they are substituted consistently. The English concept replacing x in the first factor must be identical to the x in the third premise, and so on.

Now the most spectacular form of the dilemma arises when x and z are contradictories and y and w are identical. The first example to be given will be the full standard form, and the fireworks will come later.

If a dog is the best pet for a boy, and a cat is the best pet for a girl, and if the child next door is either a boy or a girl, the child should get either a cat or a dog. Not very spectacular, is it?

But throw in a few negatives and we get:

If this man were wise, he would not speak irreverently of the Scripture in jest; and if he were good, he would not do so in earnest; therefore, he is either not wise or not good.

Or, both of course; for the *or* is *vel*, and means one or the other or both.

Now, try this familiar argument, one that has been used in many situations since it was first recorded:

Keep away from these men and let them alone; for if this plan or this work is of men, it will come to nothing; but if it is of God, you cannot overthrow it, lest you even be found to fight against God.

First, try to put this argument in symbolic form to determine its validity. Then test the premises to see if they are acceptable. The argument can be valid, even if the premises are false. For example, suppose as the Roman Catholics were massacring fifty thousand Huguenots on St. Bartholomew's Eve, someone came to Henry of Navarre and said: Don't send your army to protect the Huguenots, for if the massacre is the work of men, it will come to naught ... etc.

While Gamaliel's advice saved the Christians from some immediate persecution, it is strange that many Christians have thought him so wise.

Here is another philosophical argument you can sharpen your wits on: If the world was created, an infinite time must have elapsed before creation; and if the world was not created, an infinite time must have elapsed before the present moment; but an infinite time cannot elapse; therefore the world was neither created nor uncreated.

More on a student level is this one: If a student is fond of learning, he needs no stimulus; if he dislikes learning, a stimulus will be of no use; therefore, the instructor should apply no stimulation.

Now, finally, the fireworks, which happen to be ancient Greek fire. It is the story of Corax (the Greek name means Mr. Crow) and Tisias. Corax was a famous lawyer and Tisias became his pupil. The tuition was arranged on the following condition: If after graduation Tisias won his first case in court, he was to pay Corax a certain sum of money; but if Tisias lost his first case, there would be no charge. After graduation Tisias refused to practice law. He did not take a first case. But Corax was not stupid. He sued Tisias in court, and so Tisias involuntarily had his first case. Standing before the judge Corax argued: Your honor, I do not care how you decide this case, for if you rule in my favor I shall get my money by the order of the court; on the other hand, if you decide in favor of Tisias, he shall have won his first case, and by terms of the contract he must pay me my fee.

Now, Tisias wasn't stupid either. He had learned his lessons well, so he addressed the judge: Your honor, I do not care how you decide this case, for if you decide in my favor I shall not have to pay by order of the court. But if you decide in favor of Corax, I shall have lost my first case, and by the terms of the contract, I do not have to pay.

The judge's decision was κακοῦ κόρακος κακόν ὠόν .

While you wait to find someone to translate this untranslatable Greek pun for you, analyze the two arguments on your own. You may also consult a lawyer, but lawyers are apt to take all the fun out of it.

There are (among others) two possible mistakes a person can make in using a dilemma. The first is nothing new. The formula assumes that the first two premises are valid inferences. If one is not, the dilemma fails. This was Gamaliel's mistake. He had argued, if it be of men, it will come to naught. This does not follow. In some cases, the evil actions of men are frustrated in a short time; in other cases in a longer time. Hitler, for example, was eventually defeated. But in the meantime many people perished. Chamberlain should have resisted the takeover of Czechoslovakia, or France should have prevented the rearming of the Saar. Hitler was indeed defeated; but the results of his evil program were not naught. Therefore one should make sure that the first two premises are valid.

Another example is as follows: If the doctrines of Calvin are Scriptural, they need not be further published, for the Scriptures are already public; if, however, they are not Scriptural, they should not be published, for they would in this case be false; but either they are Scriptural or not, and in either case they should not be published.

The second and perhaps more frequent blunder, perhaps also the harder to detect, has to do with the third premise. It is a disjunction. One must make sure that it is a complete disjunction; that is, one must make certain that there is no third possibility.

Sometimes logicians wax literary and picture a dilemma as a bull. The bull bends his head and rushes at you with his horns. Then the brilliant torreador passes between the horns avoiding being impaled on either one. It is best, however, to confine bulls and torreadors to literary imagination. Clear thinking avoids such deceptive language by using phrases such as complete disjunction or incomplete disjunction.

A stupid, artificial example, without the least literary flavor would be: If I vote the Democratic ticket, I shall encourage war and inflation; if I vote Republican, I encourage depression and unemployment; but I must vote either Democratic or Republican, so I am forced to encourage war or unemployment.

Although in the United States third parties are almost uniformly useless, their mere existence makes this dilemma defective. For that matter, until we are compelled to vote whether we want to or not, we can simply refuse to go to the polls. This equally well refutes the dilemma, and it just might be more effective politically than third parties are.

Students may find the next example, equally artificial and almost as stupid, more within the range of their interests. The faculty should not offer prizes or high grades to the students, for the good students do not need such stimuli, and the poor students are allergic to any and all stimuli.

The unexpressed disjunction in this dilemma is: Students are either good or bad. But many students are in between and are susceptible to stimulation and capable of improvement.

The last section of this chapter will now concern itself with a relationship between conjunction and disjunction, and a relationship between either of these and implication. Symbolically it is this:

$$(x + y) = (x'y')' = (x' < y).$$

This short line of three factors requires a paragraph or

two in English. That is why symbolism is so useful. Several paragraphs can be expressed in one short line. And of course *x*, *y*, and *z* are not equivocal as English words often are.

Here the first two factors of the symbolism mean that if one or the other must be true, they both cannot be false. If we wrote it:

$$(xy)' = (x' + y')$$

we could say, the denial of a conjunction is the disjunction of its two terms separately denied. Or the denial of a disjunction is the conjunction of its two terms separately denied, for if you deny that either *x* or *y* is true, you are asserting that both are false:

$$(x + y)' = (x'y').$$

Next, since a disjunction asserts that at least one of its parts is true, the falsity of one part implies the truth of the other:

$$(x + y) = (x' < y) = (y' < x).$$

Thus we have this formula:

$$(x + y) = (x' < y) = (x'y')'.$$

Now, first try a few easy exercises. Turn the disjunction, "Either the student is bright or he is lucky" into an implication. Turn this conjunction into a disjunction: "The student is both stupid and lazy." Now figure up some example that fits a situation in your own school.

But finally do your best with the following well known verse. Express it as a disjunction, conjunction, and implication:

"Of making many books there is no end, and much study is wearisome to the flesh."

A student can hardly do this if he relies only on English. The present writer has had students who produce a translation that is the precise contradictory of the Scriptural verse, and yet think the two mean the same thing. The symbolism may not seem easy at first glance; there may have to be hyphenated negative terms. There will certainly be negative propositions; but the symbolism is a lot easier than ordinary English. A simple b' or (a' < b)' is easier to trace through an argument than "it is false that books are not endless implies that study is wearisome." Is that really what the verse means or is it a wrong translation?

CHAPTER 10
TRUTH TABLES

Among scholars there is some difference of opinion relative to the systematic position of truth tables in logic. They may be considered basic, from which all other formulas are derived; or they may be considered as summaries useful, like Euler's diagrams, for easy solutions to complicated problems. When the college student gets to graduate school, he may enjoy this debate. But here truth tables will be simply an easy method for disentangling complexities.

The source of all truth tables lies in the simple fact that every proposition is either true or false. And the simplest truth table is:

p	p'
T	F
F	T

which means that when p is true, p' is false, and when p is false p' is true. It will come as a surprise how such an obvious triviality can disentangle complexities almost unmanageable in English.

Two other simple truth tables represent, first, conjunction; second, disjunction:

p	q	pq
T	T	T
T	F	F
F	T	F
F	F	F

The first two columns represent every possible combination of two propositions relative to their being true or false. That is to say, in the first combination both p and q are true; in the second combination p is true and q is false. The third column shows whether or not the conjunction pq is true in the four instances. When columns one and two both show T, the pq is true; when at the bottom, p and q are each false, then pq is false. Observe also that the conjunction pq is also false in lines two and three. Naturally! The combination cannot be true unless both p and q are true individually. This is so easy, it seems like wasting space to point it out. The next one is just as easy.

p	q	p + q
T	T	T
T	F	T
F	T	T
F	F	F

The disjunction $p + q$ is true in any one where either p or q is true; and hence can be false only in line four where p and q are both false.

103

Another easy truth table concerns implication:

p	q	p < q
T	T	T
T	F	F
F	T	T
F	F	T

The first line reads: When p and q are both true, $p < q$ is valid. The second line is, when p is true and q is false, p does not imply q. Lines three and four indicate two more cases of validity.

Of course, when we talk about p and q, we refer to categorical propositions, and the rule still stands that the conclusion can contain no term not already in the premises. It is invalid to argue, Since two is an even number (T), Washington was our first president (T). At least this can be valid only in a thoroughgoing Hegelianism with which we have nothing to do here.

Now let us try a somewhat complicated problem in chemistry. First, the English argument:

Chemical compound x contains either hydrogen or silicon, but not both. It has either lithium or no hydrogen. If it contains silicon, it must contain lithium too. And if it contains lithium, it also contains hydrogen. What does this x contain, and what not?

Note that there are three chemicals involved, l, h, and s. We must first determine all the possible combinations of l, h, and s, relative to their being contained, that is, true or false. Three elements each with two values mean 2^3 or eight possibilities. These are set down in the first three columns of the following table. It is easy to construct such columns no matter how many elements there are. If it is 2^4, you simply divide the first column in half and put T's in each of the upper eight squares, and F's in the lower eight. Then divide the second column into fours, the third column into two's, and the fourth column will alternate the T's and F's. The problem we are working on has only three elements, and hence eight lines.

l	h	s	h+s	(hs)'	l+h'	s<l	l<h
T	T	T	T	F	T	T	T
T	T	F	T	T	T	T	T
T	F	T	T	T	T	T	F
T	F	F	F	T	T	T	F
F	T	T	T	F	F	F	T
F	T	F	T	T	F	T	T
F	F	T	T	T	T	F	T
F	F	F	F	T	T	T	T

The first sentence of the problem stated in English was a compound sentence, and hence was two propositions. These two are represented in columns four and five. Note the first line of the table. The three elements are all true, that is, all contained in the chemical compound. On this condition (h+s) is true and (hs)' is false. The latter is false because on line one the compound does contain both h and s. The second English sentence (the third proposition), namely, it has either lithium or no hydrogen, is represented in column six. This condition is met on lines one to four, is false on lines five and six, and is true on lines seven and eight. The student can now easily understand under what conditions (s<l) is true, and under what conditions (l<h) is true. These are columns seven and eight.

Such are all the possibilities. But what are the actualities of the English problem? That is to ask, on what lines are columns four to eight inclusive all true?

The answer is line two alone. Only line two fits all the conditions of the English problem. Hence the chemical compound contains lithium and hydrogen, but no silicon. Isn't chemistry easy!

Now, let us try another English problem.

Tom is not good in both history and science. Either he is good in logic or bad in history. If he is good in science, he is good in logic. If he is good in logic, he is good in history. What do these four premises imply; is Tom good in anything? In what?

Ooops! This is another English problem, but it is precisely the same logical problem. Instead of hydrogen we have history; instead of silicon we have science; and instead of lithium we have logic.

Here is another example, but the student must construct the table for himself.

Either D. L. Moody was a successful evangelist or Billy Sunday was a failure. If Billy Sunday was not a failure, Billy Graham is. Either D. L. Moody was not a failure or Billy Graham is not. If Billy Sunday was a failure, then Billy Graham is not.

Here is a different and final example. Either the birds are singing or the baby is crying. If the baby is not crying, then the wind is blowing. Either the birds are not singing or the wind is not blowing. Are the birds singing? Is the baby crying? Is the wind blowing? The first three columns are always the same. Since the second condition of the problem contains a negative, we shall insert a fifth column to avoid confusion. The student can insert another such column for the negative in the third and fourth columns if he wishes.

a	b	c	a+b	b'	b'<c	a'+c'	b<c'
T	T	T	T	F	T	F	F
T	T	F	T	F	T	T	T
T	F	T	T	T	T	F	T
T	F	F	T	T	F	T	T
F	T	T	T	F	T	T	F
F	T	F	T	F	T	T	T
F	F	T	F	T	T	T	T
F	F	F	F	T	F	T	T

After checking the table to see that the publisher made no typographical errors that the proofreaders did not catch, the student will note that lines two and six, and those only, represent the conditions of the problem. Now you must look back to the first three columns and find what is true in every case. Since line two says the birds are singing, and line six says they are not, we cannot say anything about the birds. But note that the baby is crying both times. Note also that the wind is not blowing in lines two and six. This then is the solution to the problem.

CHAPTER 11
THE DEDUCTION OF THE SYLLOGISM

In the chapter on the syllogism Barbara and Celarent were treated as axioms and the other twenty-two were theorems deduced from these two. But it is not necessary to use Barbara and Celarent as axioms. They also can be theorems deduced from still simpler assumptions.

The trick is to develop Barbara from the law of transitivity. We assume (a<b) (b<c) < (a<c). Of course we could write this (x<y) (y<z) < (x<z); or as (b<a) (a<c) < (b<c). These are not three assumptions. They are a single one, only that the terms are different. It makes no difference whether we say "the class cats is included in the class mammals; the class mammals is included in the class animals; therefore, the class cats is included in the class animals"; or whether we say, "Athenians are included in Greeks; Greeks are included in Europeans; therefore, the class Athenians is included in the class Europeans."

With this principle in mind we are permitted to write the law of transitivity in six different ways:

(1) (c < b) (b < a) < (c < a).

Now since this procedure will take up some space and will be a little tedious, it will save printers' ink if we simply omit the inclusion signs and write our formulas as follows:

(1)	cb	ba	<	ca
(2)	ab	bc	<	ac
(3)	bc	(ba')'	<	(ca')'

Note that this third line comes, by contradiction and interchange, from bc ca'<ba', which is itself an evident form of transitivity:

$$
\begin{array}{llll}
(4) & (a'b)' & cb & < & (a'c)' \\
(5) & ba & (bc')' & < & (ac')' \\
(6) & (c'b)' & ab & < & (c'a)'.
\end{array}
$$

The derivation of the syllogism from the law of transitivity, expressed these six ways, may be tedious, but with one exception is very easily followed.

First, multiply both sides of lines one and two.
Second, multiply both sides of lines one, three, and four.
Third, the same for lines one, five and six.
Fourth, the same for lines one, four and five. But now attach to the antecedent here the factors (ba')' and (c'b)'.

Now, add all these four together, as follows:

I. cb ba ab bc < ca ac
II. cb ba bc (ba')' (a'b)' cb < ca (ca')' (a'c)'
III. cb ba ba (bc')' (c'b)' ab < ca (ac')' (c'a)'
IV. cb ba (a'b)' cb ba (bc')' (ba')' (c'b)' < ca (ac)' (ac')'.

These are the four expressions which must be added. Since the sum of the antecedents would make a long line, we shall add the conclusions first:

ca ac + ca(ca')'(a'c)'+ ca(ac')'(c'a)'+ ca(a'c)'(ac')'.

Note that ca occurs in every one of the four factors and hence may be factored out:

ca[ac + (ca')'(a'c)' + (ac')'(c'a)' + (a'c)'(ac')']

Now look at the last two parentheses, the last two factors at the end of the brackets. Note that they, (a'c)' (ac')', are the same as the previous two, (ac')'(c'a)'. The (ac')' looks identical; the other two are identical also because by contradiction and interchange (a'c)=(c'a)'. Hence we may drop the last two factors in the brackets because there is no use in saying the same thing twice. In a syllogism we would not have three premises, two of which were All dogs are animals and All non-animals are non-dogs. Once is enough.

Now, note for the same reason that the middle two parentheses are redundant because they, (ac')' (c'a)' = (ca')' (a'c)'. That is,

$$(ac')' = (ca')' \text{ and}$$
$$(c'a)' = (a'c)'.$$

Hence the addition of the conclusions in the four implications, numbered I, II, III, IV, reduces to

$$(c<a) \; [(a <c) + (c<a')' \; (a'<c)'].$$

And this is the definition, as previously given, of A(ca), the conclusion of Barbara.

If now we add the four antecedents, the result will be the product of the definitions of A(ba) and A(cb). Remember that implication IV had two factors inserted (multiplied) into its antecedent. The justification for this sleight of hand is this: If $xy<z$, then $xypqr<z$. The p, q, r may be unneccessary, but their insertion does not affect the validity of the implication. Therefore, the premises of Barbara are more than enough to imply its conclusion. Thus Barbara is a deduction from the law of transitivity, and the other twenty-two can come as previously explained. In this way logic is simplified by deducing more conclusions from fewer axioms.

Granted that nearly all contemporary logicians will reject our symbolization of A(ab), yet it has been made clear that their definition does not express the English meaning of *All dogs are animals*. But further study is on a higher level than this textbook.

In conclusion, the student should remember, for the rest of his life, that if he is logical, he will never go wrong—unless he starts with false premises. Logic will not guarantee the truth of the premises, but without logic no progress is possible.

POSTSCRIPT
GOD AND LOGIC

In thinking about God Calvinists almost immediately repeat the Shorter Catechism and say, "God is a spirit, infinite, eternal, and unchangeable." Perhaps we do not pause
to clarify our ideas of spirit, but hurry on to the attributes
of "wisdom, holiness, justice, goodness, and truth." But
pause: Spirit, Wisdom, Truth. Psalm 31:5 addresses God as
"O Lord God of *truth*." John 17:3 says, "This is life eternal,
that they might *know* thee, the only *true* God. . . . 1 John 5:6
says, "The Spirit is *truth*." Such verses as these indicate that
God is a rational, thinking being, whose thought exhibits
the structure of Aristotelian logic.

If anyone objects to Aristotelian logic in this connection —and presumably he does not want to replace it with
the Boolean-Russell symbolic logic—let him ask and answer whether it is true for God that if all dogs have teeth,
some dogs, spaniels, have teeth? Do those who contrast this
"merely human logic" with divine logic mean that for God
all dogs may have teeth while spaniels do not? Similarly,
with "merely human" arithmetic: Two plus two is four for
man, but is it eleven for God? Ever since Bernard distrusted
Abelard, it has been a mark of piety, in some quarters, to
disparage "mere human reason"; and at the present time
existentialistic neo-orthodox authors object to "straight-
line" inference and insist that faith must "curb" logic. Thus
they not only refuse to make logic an axiom, but reserve
the right to repudiate it. In opposition to this latter view

the following argument will continue to insist on the necessity of logic; and with respect to the contention that Scripture cannot be axiomatic because logic must be, it will be necessary to spell out in greater detail the meaning of Scriptural revelation.

Now, since in this context verbal revelation is a revelation from God, the discussion will begin with the relation between God and logic. Afterward will come the relation between logic and the Scriptures. And finally the discussion will turn to logic in man.

Logic and God

It will be best to begin by calling attention to some of the characteristics the Scriptures attribute to God. Nothing startling is involved in remarking that God is omniscient. This is a commonplace of Christian theology. But, further, God is eternally omniscient. He has not learned his knowledge. And since God exists of himself, independent of everything else, indeed the Creator of everything else, he must himself be the source of his own knowledge. This important point has had a history.

At the beginning of the Christian era, Philo, the Jewish scholar of Alexandria, made an adjustment in Platonic philosophy to bring it into accord with the theology of the Old Testament. Plato had based his system on three original, independent principles: the World of Ideas, the Demiurge, and chaotic space. Although the three were equally eternal and independent of each other, the Demiurge fashioned chaotic space into this visible world by using the Ideas as his model. Hence in Plato the World of Ideas is not only independent of but even in a sense superior to the maker of Heaven and Earth. He is morally obligated, and in fact willingly submits, to the Ideas of justice, man, equality, and number.

Philo, however, says, "God has been ranked according

to the one and the unit; or rather even the unit has been ranked according to the one God, for all number, like time, is younger than the cosmos, while God is older than the cosmos and its creator."

This means that God is the source and determiner of all truth. Christians generally, even uneducated Christians, understand that water, milk, alcohol, and gasoline freeze at different temperatures because God created them that way. God could have made an intoxicating fluid freeze at zero Fahrenheit, and he could have made the cow's product freeze at forty. But he decided otherwise. Therefore behind the act of creation there is an eternal decree. It was God's eternal purpose to have such liquids, and therefore we can say that the particularities of nature were determined before there was any nature.

Similarly in all other varieties of truth, God must be accounted sovereign. It is his decree that makes one proposition true and another false. Whether the proposition be physical, psychological, moral or theological, it is God who made it that way. A proposition is true because God thinks it so.

Perhaps for a certain formal completeness a sample of Scriptural documentation might be appropriate. Psalm 147:5 says that "God is our Lord, and of great power; his understanding is infinite." If we cannot strictly conclude from this verse that God's power is the origin of his understanding, at least there is no doubt that omniscience is asserted. 1 Samuel 2:3 says that "the Lord is a God of knowledge." Ephesians 1:8 speaks of God's wisdom and prudence. In Romans 16:27 we have the phrase, "God only wise," and 1 Timothy 1:17 the similar phrase, "the only wise God."

Further references and an excellent exposition of them may be found in Stephen Charnock, *The Existence and Attributes of God*, chapters VII and IX. From this distinguished author a few lines must be included here.

"God knows himself because his knowledge with his will is the cause of all other things; . . . he is the first truth, and therefore is the first object of his understanding. . . . As he is all knowledge, so he hath in himself the most excellent object of knowledge. . . . No object is so intelligible to God as God is to himself . . . for his understanding is his essence, himself." Then a few pages later: "God knows his own decree and will, and therefore must know all things. . . . God must know what he hath decreed to come to pass. . . . God must know because he willed them . . . he therefore knows them because he knows what he willed. The knowledge of God cannot rise from the things themselves, for then the knowledge of God would have a cause without him. . . . As God sees things possible in the glass of his own power, so he sees things future in the glass of his own will."

A great deal of Charnock's material has as its purpose the listing of the objects of God's knowledge. Here, however, the quotations were made to point out that God's knowledge depends on his will and on nothing external to him. Thus we may repeat with Philo that God is not to be ranked under the idea of unity, or of goodness, or of truth; but rather unity, goodness, and truth are to be ranked under the decree of God.

Logic Is God

It is to be hoped that these remarks on the relation between God and truth will be seen as pertinent to the discussion of logic. In any case, the subject of logic can be more clearly introduced by one more Scriptural reference. The well-known prologue to John's Gospel may be paraphrased, "In the beginning was Logic, and Logic was with God, and Logic was God. . . . In Logic was life and the life was the light of men."

This paraphrase, in fact, this translation, may not only sound strange to devout ears, it may even sound obnoxious and offensive. But the shock only measures the devout person's distance from the language and thought of the Greek New Testament. Why it is offensive to call Christ Logic, when it does not offend to call him a Word, is hard to explain. But such is often the case. Even Augustine, because he insisted that God is truth, has been subjected to the anti-intellectualistic accusation of "reducing" God to a proposition. At any rate, the strong intellectualism of the word *Logos* is seen in its several possible translations: to wit, computation, (financial) accounts, esteem, proportion and (mathematical) ratio, explanation, theory or argument, principle or law, reason, formula, debate, narrative, speech, deliberation, discussion, oracle, sentence, and wisdom.

Any translation of John 1:1 that obscures this emphasis on mind or reason is a bad translation. And if anyone complains that the idea of *ratio* or debate obscures the personality of the second person of the Trinity, he should alter his concept of personality. In the beginning, then, was Logic.

That Logic is the light of men is a proposition that could well introduce the section after next on the relation of logic to man. But the thought that Logic is God will bring us to the conclusion of the present section. Not only do the followers of Bernard entertain suspicions about logic, but even more systematic theologians are wary of any proposal that would make an abstract principle superior to God. The present argument, in consonance with both Philo and Charnock, does not do so. The law of contradiction is not to be taken as an axiom prior to or independent of God. The law is God thinking.

For this reason also the law of contradiction is not subsequent to God. If one should say that logic is dependent on God's thinking, it is dependent only in the sense that it is the characteristic of God's thinking. It is not subsequent temporally, for God is eternal and there was never a time when God existed without thinking logically. One must not suppose that God's will existed as an inert substance before he willed to think.

As there is no temporal priority, so also there is no logical or analytical priority. Not only was Logic the beginning, but Logic was God. If this unusual translation of John's Prologue still disturbs someone, he might yet allow that God is his thinking. God is not a passive or potential substratum; he is actuality or activity. This is the philosophical terminology to express the Biblical idea that God is a living God. Hence logic is to be considered as the activity of God's willing.

Although Aristotle's theology is no better, and perhaps worse, than his epistemology, he used a phrase to describe God, which with a slight change, may prove helpful. He defined God as "thought-thinking-thought." Aristotle developed the meaning of this phrase so as to deny divine omniscience. But if we are clear that the thought which thought thinks includes thought about a world to be created—in Aristotle God has no knowledge of things inferior to him—the Aristotelian definition of God as "thought-thinking-thought" may help us to understand that logic, the law of contradiction, is neither prior to nor subsequent to God's activity.

This conclusion may disturb some analytical thinkers. They may wish to separate logic and God. Doing so, they would complain that the present construction merges two axioms into one. And if two, one of them must be prior; in which case we would have to accept God without logic, or logic without God; and the other one afterward. But this is not the presupposition here proposed. God and logic are one and the same first principle, for John wrote that Logic was God.

At the moment this much must suffice to indicate the relation of God to logic. We now pass to what at the beginning seemed to be the more pertinent question of logic and Scripture.

Logic and Scripture

There is a minor misunderstanding that can easily be disposed of before discussing the relation of logic to the Scriptures. Someone with a lively historical sense might wonder why Scripture and revelation are equated, when God's direct speech to Moses, Samuel, and the prophets is even more clearly revelation.

This observation became possible simply because of previous brevity. Of course God's speech to Moses was revelation, in fact, revelation *par excellence*, if you wish. But we are not Moses. Therefore, if the problem is to explain how we know in this age, one cannot use the personal experience of Moses. Today we have the Scripture. As the Westminster Confession says, "It pleased the Lord . . . to reveal himself . . . and afterwards . . . to commit the same wholly unto writing, which makes the Holy Scripture to be most necessary, those former ways of God's revealing his will unto his people being now ceased." What God said to Moses is written in the Bible; the words are identical; the revelation is the same.

In this may be anticipated the relation of logic to the Scripture. First of all, Scripture, the written words of the Bible, is the mind of God. What is said in Scripture is God's thought.

In contemporary religious polemics the Biblical view of the Bible, the historic position of the Reformation, or, what is the same thing, the doctrine of plenary and verbal inspiration is castigated as bibliolatry. The liberals accuse the Lutherans and Calvinists of worshiping a book instead of worshiping God. Apparently they think that we genuflect to the Bible on the pulpit, and they deride us for kissing the ring of a paper pope.

This caricature stems from their materialistic turn of mind, a materialism that may not be apparent in other discussions, but which comes to the surface when they direct their fire against fundamentalism. They think of the Bible as a material book, with paper contents, and a leather binding. That the contents are the thoughts of God, expressed in God's own words, is a position to which they are so invincibly antagonistic that they cannot even admit it to be the position of a fundamentalist.

Nevertheless we maintain that the Bible expresses the mind of God. Conceptually it is the mind of God, or, more accurately, a part of God's mind. For this reason the Apostle Paul, referring to the revelation given him, and in fact given to the Corinthians through him, is able to say, "We have the mind of Christ." Also in Philippians 2:5 he exhorts them, "Let this mind be in you which was also in Christ Jesus." To the same purpose is his modest claim in 1 Corinthians 7:40, "I think also that I have the Spirit of God."

The Bible then is the mind or thought of God. It is not a physical fetish, like a crucifix. And I doubt that there has ever been even one hillbilly fundamentalist ignorant enough to pray to a black book with red edges. Similarly, the charge that the Bible is a paper pope misses the mark for the same reason. The Bible consists of thoughts, not paper; and the thoughts are the thoughts of the omniscient, infallible God, not those of Innocent III.

On this basis, that is, on the basis that Scripture is the mind of God, the relation to logic can easily be made clear. As might be expected, if God has spoken, he has spoken logically. The Scripture therefore should and does exhibit logical organization.

For example, Romans 4:2 is an enthymematic hypothetical destructive syllogism. Romans 5:13 is a hypothetical constructive syllogism. 1 Corinthians 15:15-18 is a sorites. Obviously, examples of standard logical forms such as these could be listed at great length.

There is of course much in Scripture that is not syllogistic. The historical sections are largely narrative. Yet every declarative sentence is a logical unit. These sentences are truths; as such they are objects of knowledge. Each of them has, or perhaps we should say, each of them is a predicate attached to a subject. Only so can they convey meaning.

Even in the single words themselves, as is most clearly seen in the cases of nouns and verbs, logic is embedded. If Scripture says, David was King of Israel, it does not mean that David was president of Babylon; and surely it does not mean that Churchill was prime minister of China. That is to say, the words *David*, *King*, and *Israel* have definite meanings.

The old libel that Scripture is a wax nose and that interpretation is infinitely elastic is clearly wrong. If there were no limits to interpretation, we might interpret the libel itself as an acceptance of verbal and plenary inspiration. But since the libel cannot be so interpreted, neither can the virgin birth be interpreted as a myth nor the resurrection as a symbol of spring. No doubt there are some things hard to be understood which the unlearned wrest to their own destruction, but the difficulties are no greater than those found in Aristotle or Plotinus, and against these philosophers no such libel is ever directed. Furthermore, only some things are hard. For the rest, Protestants have insisted on the perspicuity of Scripture.

Nor need we waste time repeating Aristotle's explanation of ambiguous words. The fact that a word must mean one thing and not its contradictory is the evidence of the law of contradiction in all rational language.

This exhibition of the logic embedded in Scripture explains why Scripture rather than the law of contradiction is selected as the axiom. Should we assume merely the law of contradiction, we would be no better off than Kant was. His notion that knowledge requires *a priori* categories deserves great respect. Once for all, in a positive way—the complement of Hume's negative and unintentional way—

Kant demonstrated the necessity of axioms, presuppositions, or *a priori* equipment. But this *sine qua non* is not sufficient to produce knowledge. Therefore the law of contradiction as such and by itself is not made the axiom of this argument.

For a similar reason, God as distinct from Scripture is not made the axiom of this argument. Undoubtedly this twist will seem strange to many theologians. It will seem particularly strange after the previous emphasis on the mind of God as the origin of all truth. Must not God be the axiom? For example, the first article of the Augsburg Confession gives the doctrine of God, and the doctrine of the Scripture is discussed in the next five. The Belgic Confession has the same order. The Scotch Confession of 1560 begins with God and gets to the Scripture only in article nineteen. The Thirty-Nine Articles begin with the Trinity, and Scripture comes in articles six and following. If God is sovereign, it seems very reasonable to put him first in the system.

But several other creeds, and especially the Westminster Confession, state the doctrine of Scripture at the very start. The explanation is quite simple: Our knowledge of God comes from the Bible. We may assert that every proposition is true because God thinks it so, and we may follow Charnock in all his great detail, but the whole is based on Scripture. Suppose this were not so. Then "God" as an axiom, apart from Scripture, is just a name. We must specify which God. The best known system in which "God" was made the axiom is Spinoza's. For him all theorems are deduced from *Deus sive Natura*. But it is the *Natura* that identifies Spinoza's god. Different gods might be made axioms of other systems. Hence the important thing is not to presuppose God, but to define the mind of the God presupposed. Therefore the Scripture is offered here as the axiom. This gives definiteness and content, without which axioms are useless.

Thus it is that God, Scripture, and logic are tied together.

121

The pietists should not complain that emphasis on logic is a deification of an abstraction, or of human reason divorced from God. Emphasis on logic is strictly in accord with John's Prologue and is nothing other than recognition of the nature of God.

Does it seem peculiar, in this connection, that a theologian can be so greatly attached to the doctrine of the atonement, or a Pietist to the idea of sanctification, which nonetheless is explained only in some parts of Scripture, and yet be hostile to or suspicious of rationality and logic which every verse of Scripture exhibits?

Logic in Man

With this understanding of God's mind, the next step is the creation of man in God's image. The non-rational animals were not created in his image; but God breathed his spirit into the earthly form and Adam became a type of soul superior to the animals.

To be precise, one should not speak of the image of God in man. Man is not something in which somewhere God's image can be found along with other things. Man *is* the image. This, of course, does not refer to man's body. The body is an instrument or tool man uses. He himself is God's breath, the spirit God breathed into the clay, the mind, the thinking ego. Therefore, man is rational in the likeness of God's rationality. His mind is structured as Aristotelian logic described it. That is why we believe that spaniels have teeth.

In addition to the well known verses in chapter one, Genesis 5:1 and 9:6 both repeat the idea. 1 Corinthians 11:7 says that "man . . . is the image and glory of God." See also Colossians 3:10 and James 3:9. Other verses, not so explicit, nonetheless add to our information. Compare Hebrews 1:3, Hebrews 2:6-8, and Psalm 8. But the conclusive consideration is that throughout the Bible as a whole the rational God gives man an intelligible message.

It is strange that anyone who thinks he is a Christian should deprecate logic. Such a person does not of course intend to deprecate the mind of God; but he thinks that logic in man is sinful, even more sinful than other parts of man's fallen nature. This, however, makes no sense. The law of contradiction cannot be sinful. Quite the contrary, it is our violations of the law of contradiction that are sinful. Yet the strictures which some devotional writers place on "merely human" logic are amazing. Can such pious stupidity really mean that a syllogism which is valid for us is invalid for God? If two plus two is four in our arithmetic, does God have a different arithmetic in which two and two makes three or perhaps five?

The fact that the Son of God is God's reason, for Christ is the wisdom of God as well as the power of God, plus the fact that the image in man is so-called "human reason," suffices to show that this so-called "human reason" is not so much human as divine.

Of course, the Scripture says that God's thoughts are not our thoughts and his ways are not our ways. But is it good exegesis to say that this means his logic, his arithmetic, his truth are not ours? If this were so, what would the consequences be? It would mean not only that our additions and subtractions are all wrong, but also that all our thoughts, in history as well as in arithmetic, are all wrong. If for example, we think that David was King of Israel, and God's thoughts are not ours, then it follows that God does not think David was King of Israel. David in God's mind was perchance prime minister of Babylon.

To avoid this irrationalism, which of course is a denial of the divine image, we must insist that truth is the same for God and man. Naturally, we may not know the truth about some matters. But if we know anything at all, what we must know must be identical with what God knows. God knows all truth, and unless we know something God knows, our ideas are untrue. It is absolutely essential, therefore, to insist that there is an area of coincidence between God's mind and our mind.

Logic and Language

This point brings us to the central issue of language. Language did not develop from, nor was its purpose restricted to, the physical needs of earthly life. God gave Adam a mind to understand the divine law, and he gave him language to enable him to speak to God. From the beginning language was intended for worship. In the *Te Deum*, by means of language, and in spite of the fact that it is sung to music, we pay "metaphysical compliments" to God. The debate about the adequacy of language to express the truth of God is a false issue. Words are merely symbols or signs. Any sign would be adequate. The real issue is: Does a man have the idea to symbolize? If he can think of God, then he can use the sound *God, Deus, Theos*, or *Elohim*. The word makes no difference; the sign is *ipso facto* literal and adequate.

The Christian view is that God created Adam as a rational mind. The structure of Adam's mind was the same as God's. God thinks that asserting the consequent is a fallacy; and Adam's mind was formed on the principles of identity and contradiction. This Christian view of God, man, and language does not fit into any empirical philosophy. It is rather a type of *a priori* rationalism. Man's mind is not initially a blank. It is structured. In fact, an unstructured blank is no mind at all. Nor could any such sheet of white paper extract any universal law of logic from finite experience. No universal and necessary proposition can be deduced from sensory observation. Universality and necessity can only be *a priori*.

This is not to say that all truth can be deduced from logic alone. The seventeenth century rationalists gave themselves an impossible task. Even if the ontological argument be valid, it is impossible to deduce *Cur Deus Homo*, the Trinity, or the final resurrection. The axioms to which the *a priori* forms of logic must be applied are the propositions God revealed to Adam and the later prophets.

Conclusion

Logic is irreplaceable. It is not an arbitrary tautology, a useful framework among others. Various systems of cataloging books in libraries are possible, and several are equally convenient. They are all arbitrary. History can be designated by 800 as easily as by 500. But there is no substitute for the law of contradiction. If dog is the equivalent of not-dog, and if 2=3=4, not only do zoology and mathematics disappear, Victor Hugo and Johann Wolfgang Goethe also disappear. These two men are particularly appropriate examples, for they are both, especially Goethe, romanticists. Even so, without logic, Goethe could not have attacked the logic of John's Gospel (I, 1224-1237).

> Geschrieben steht: "Im anfang war das Wort!"
> Hier stock ich schon! Wer hilft mir weiter fort?
>
> Mir hilft der Geist! Auf einmal seh' ich Rath
> Und schreib' getrost: "Im anfang war die That!"*

But Goethe can express his rejection of the divine *Logos* of John 1:1, and express his acceptance of romantic experience, only by using the Logic he despises.

To repeat, even if it seem wearisome: Logic is fixed, universal, necessary, and irreplaceable. Irrationality contradicts the biblical teaching from beginning to end. The God of Abraham, Isaac, and Jacob is not insane. God is a rational being, the architecture of whose mind is Logic.

---

* It is written: "In the beginning was the Word!"
Here I'm stuck already! Who helps me go further?
The spirit helps me! All at once I see the answer
And confidently write: "In the beginning was the Act!"—*Editor*

GLOSSARY

Note: The numbers following each definition are the pages of the text on which fuller discussions of the terms may be found.

abusive ad hominem—An informal logical fallacy in which irrelevancies of character are used as reasons for rejecting a position. Example: Proposition x cannot be true, because y, who believes x, is a drunkard. (16)

accent—An informal logical fallacy in which the meaning of a sentence, phrase, or word is misunderstood because it is dependent on the inflection of the voice. (9-10)

accident—An informal logical fallacy in which an irrelevant, accidental factor becomes the essential point in an argument. (18)

ad baculum—Latin meaning "to the stick." An informal logical fallacy in which an appeal to force and threats is made. (18)

ad hominem—Latin meaning "to the man." A form of argument that accepts a proposition espoused by another for the purpose of deducing from it contradictory propositions or propositions that would be rejected by the other person. *Ad hominem* should be distinguished from the informal fallacy *abusive ad hominem*. (15-16)

ad populum—Latin meaning "to the people." An informal logical fallacy involving an appeal to popular opinion. (17)

affirmative form—One of four categorical forms (A, E, I,

O) of a proposition; an affirmative form does not distribute its predicate. (38-39)

ambiguity—A word susceptible of more than one meaning. (5-6)

amphibology—A phrase or sentence susceptible of more than one meaning, also spelled amphiboly. (9)

argument—A connected series of statements or reasons intended to establish a conclusion. (1)

argumentum ad misericordiam—Latin meaning "argument to mercy," it is an informal logical fallacy in which an appeal is made to the sympathy of the hearer. (17)

axiom—A first principle or premise, which, because it is first, does not need to be demonstrated and cannot be demonstrated. It is the basis of all argument and demonstration. (2)

categorical syllogism—Both "categorical" and "hypothetical" syllogisms are categorical and hypothetical: "categorical," because their forms are related to predicates or categories; "hypothetical," because logic does not assert the truth of a premise. "Hypothetical syllogism" also refers to *modus ponens* and *modus tollens*. (83-84)

category—A name given to certain general classes of terms, things, or ideas. (120)

complex question—An informal logical fallacy consisting of two or more questions or a question with two or more assumptions in it. Example: Have you stopped beating your wife yet? (17)

composition—An informal logical fallacy in which the characteristic of the part is attributed to the whole. (12-13)

conclusion—A proposition deduced by reasoning from previous propositions. (28)

connotative definition—A definition which lists the necessary and sufficient attributes of the term defined. (21)

contradiction—One of the four kinds of opposition (contradiction, contrariety , subcontrariety, subalternation); a statement containing propositions one of which denies or is logically at variance with the other; a statement or phrase which is self-contradictory on the face of it. Two contradictory propositions cannot both be true and cannot both be false. (43)

contraposition—Contradicting and interchanging the subject and predicate. A(ab) becomes A(b'a'). It is valid in the cases of A and O; invalid for E and I. (51)

contrariety—Two propositions that cannot both be true but can both be false are contraries. (43)

conversion per accidens—The process of inferring I from A or O from E in the second figure. The conclusion of Bramantip is an example. (66)

copula—That part of a proposition which connects the subject and the predicate; the present tense of the verb *to be*. (28)

denotative definition—A definition which lists the members of the term or class defined. (21)

dilemma—An argument whose conclusion follows (or seems to follow) from contradictory premises. (94)

disjunctive hypothetical syllogism—Symbolically: Either x or y; not x; therefore, y. (91)

distributed term—A term of a proposition modified by the adjectives *all* or *no*. (38)

division—An informal logical fallacy in which a characteristic of the whole is attributed to a part. (12-13)

enthymeme—An argument in which one or more of the premises is omitted or taken for granted. (3)

equivocation—A word susceptible of more than one meaning. (7)

existential import—The opinion of symbolic logic that universal statements do not imply the existence of the subject, but particular statements do. All a is b does not imply that there are any a's; but some a is b does. Particular statements have existential import; universal statements do not. Existential import is a fiction. (83)

fallacy (formal and informal)—A mistake in reasoning. An informal fallacy is a mistake in grammar or usage; a formal fallacy is a mistake in the form of the argument itself. (7)

figure—The form of an inference determined by the different positions of the terms in the premise(s) and conclusion. (49)

form—The arrangement of subject and predicate in a proposition; there are four forms: *All a is b* (A), *No a is b* (E), *Some a is b* (I), *Some a is not b* (O). Sometimes they are called categorical forms. (27)

genus—A class or kind of things which includes a number of subordinate kinds (species) as having certain attributes in common. *Plural*, genera. (24)

hypothetical syllogism—See *modus ponens* and *modus tollens*.

ignoratio elenchi—Latin meaning "ignorance of the refutation." (16)

immediate inference—An argument with one proposition as a premise and one proposition as a conclusion; there is no middle term. (32, 47)

inference—The forming of a conclusion from premises by either inductive or deductive methods; the conclusion itself. (37)

infimae species—Lowest species. (24)

law of contradiction—The same attribute cannot at the same time belong and not belong to the same subject and in the same respect. A word, in order to mean something, must also mean not-something else. (120)

logic—The science of necessary inference, *passim*.

major premise—The premise of a syllogism that contains the major term. (56)

major term—The predicate of the conclusion of an inference. (55)

metaphysics—The branch of philosophy concerned with the nature of reality. There are three other major branches: epistemology, ethics, and politics.

middle term—The term that appears in both premises of a syllogism but not in the conclusion. (56)

minor premise—The premise of a syllogism that contains the minor term. (56)

minor term—The subject of the conclusion of an inference. (55-56)

modus ponens—Latin meaning "method or way of constructing"; symbolically: If p, then q; p; therefore, q. (89)

modus tollens—Latin meaning "method or way of destroying"; symbolically: If p, then q; not q; therefore, not p. (89)

mood—An individual case of an inference. (50)

negative form—That one of four categorical forms (A, E, I, O) of a proposition which distributes its predicate. (39)

obversion—Replacing one form of a proposition with another by contradicting the predicate of the first and changing the quality of the proposition: *All a is b* by obversion becomes *No a is not-b*. (51)

ostensive definition—"Defining" a term by pointing at things—referents—to which the term refers. Augustine showed that ostensive definition is impossible. (25)

particular form—That one of four categorical forms (A, E, I, O) of a proposition which does not distribute its subject. (41)

petitio principii—Latin meaning "begging the question." It is actually a valid form of argument in which one of the premises from which the conclusion is deduced is the conclusion itself in disguised form. It is regarded as an informal logical fallacy because it is unconvincing to someone who does not accept the premise-conclusion. (14-15)

post hoc ergo propter hoc—Latin meaning "after this, therefore because of this." An informal fallacy. (17)

premise—A proposition of an argument from which a conclusion is obtained. (2)

proposition—A form of words in which something (the predicate) is affirmed or denied of something (the subject); the meaning expressed by a declarative sentence. (28)

reductio ad impossible—Latin meaning "reduce to the impossible." The process of deducing a conclusion known to be false from a given premise, thus demonstrating the falsity of the premise. (66)

reflexive relationship—A relationship that holds between one of its objects and that object itself. Equality in arithmetic and implication in logic are reflexive relationships. (41)

sentence—A series of words in connected speech or writing forming the grammatically complete expression of a single thought. (27)

simple conversion—The transposition of the subject and predicate of a proposition to form a new proposition: *No a is b* becomes *No b is a*. (51)

sorites—A series of propositions in which the predicate of each is the subject of the next, the conclusion being formed of the first subject and last predicate. (86)

species—A class composed of individuals having some common qualities or characteristics. (24)

subalternation—One of the four kinds of opposition (contradiction, contrariety, subcontrariety, subalternation); the opposition that exists between propositions alike in quality but different in quantity: subalterns may both be true and may both be false. (43)

subcontrariety—One of the four kinds of opposition (contradiction, contrariety, subcontrariety, subalternation); the opposition that exists between propositions alike in quantity but different in quality. Subcontrary propositions cannot both be false but can both be true. (43)

syllogism—An argument composed of two premises and a conclusion, with the predicate of the conclusion in one, the subject of the conclusion in the other, and a third term in the two premises. There are 256 possible moods of syllogisms. (55)

symmetrical relationship—A relationship which, if it holds between two objects, *a* and *b*, also holds between *b* and *a*. *Cousin* is a symmetrical relationship. *Father* is not. (41)

term—Each of the words denoting a thing or idea in a proposition; the subject or predicate of any of the propositions composing a syllogism, forming one of its three elements (major term, minor term, middle term) each of which occurs twice.

theorem—A proposition deduced from an axiom. (2)

transitive relationship—A relationship is transitive if, when it holds between two of its objects, *a* and *b*, and also between *b* and *c*, holds as well between *a* and *c*. (42)

tree of Porphyry—An ancient method for defining terms by a series of dichotomies. (23)

undistributed term—A term of a proposition not modified by the adjectives *all* or *no*. (38)

universal form—Those of the four categorical forms (A, E, I, O) of a proposition which distribute their subject. (41)

univocal—Having one meaning. (11)

valid—A quality of arguments in which the conclusion necessarily results from the premises; an argument is valid if the form of the conclusion is true every time the forms of the premises are true. (32-33)

INDEX

Scripture Index

THE CRISIS OF OUR TIME

Historians have christened the thirteenth century the Age of Faith and termed the eighteenth century the Age of Reason. The present age has been called many things: the Atomic Age, the Age of Inflation, the Age of the Tyrant, the Age of Aquarius; but it deserves one name more than the others: the Age of Irrationalism. Contemporary secular intellectuals are anti-intellectual. Contemporary philosophers are anti-philosophy. Contemporary theologians are anti-theology.

In past centuries, secular philosophers have generally believed that knowledge is possible to man. Consequently they expended a great deal of thought and effort trying to justify knowledge. In the twentieth century, however, the optimism of the secular philosophers all but disappeared. They despaired of knowledge.

Like their secular counterparts, the great theologians and doctors of the church taught that knowledge is possible to man. Yet the theologians of the present age also repudiated that belief. They too despaired of knowledge. This radical skepticism has penetrated our entire culture, from television to music to literature. *The Christian at the beginning of the twenty-first century is confronted with an overwhelming cultural consensus – sometimes stated explicitly but most often implicitly: Man does not and cannot know anything truly.*

What does this have to do with Christianity? Simply this: If man can know nothing truly, man can truly know nothing. We cannot know that the Bible is the Word of God, that Christ

141

died for his people, or that Christ is alive today at the right hand of the Father. Unless knowledge is possible, Christianity is nonsensical, for it claims to be knowledge. What is at stake at the beginning of the twenty-first century is not simply a single doctrine, such as the virgin birth, or the existence of Hell, as important as those doctrines may be, but the whole of Christianity itself. If knowledge is not possible to man, it is worse than silly to argue points of doctrine – it is insane.

The irrationalism of the present age is so thoroughgoing and pervasive that even the Remnant – the segment of the professing church that remains faithful – has accepted much of it, frequently without even being aware of what it is accepting. In some religious circles this irrationalism has become synonymous with piety and humility, and those who oppose it are denounced as rationalists, as though to be logical were a sin. Our contemporary anti-theologians make a contradiction and call it a Mystery. The faithful ask for truth and are given Paradox and Antinomy. If any balk at swallowing the absurdities of the anti-theologians who teach in the seminaries or have graduated from the seminaries, they are frequently marked as heretics or schismatics who seek to act independently of God.

There is no greater threat facing the church of Christ at this moment than the irrationalism that now controls our entire culture. Totalitarianism, guilty of tens of millions of murders – including those of millions of Christians – is to be feared, but not nearly so much as the idea that we do not and cannot know the literal truth. Hedonism, the popular philosophy of America, is not to be feared so much as the belief that logic – that "mere human logic," to use the religious irrationalists' own phrase – is futile. The attacks on truth, on knowledge, on propositional revelation, on the intellect, on words, and on logic are renewed daily. But note well: The misologists – the haters of logic – use logic to demonstrate the futility of using logic. The anti-intellectuals construct intricate intellectual arguments to prove the insufficiency of the intellect. Those who deny the competence of words to express thought use words to express their thoughts. The proponents of poetry, myth, metaphor, and analogy argue for their theories by using literal prose, whose competence – even whose possibility – they deny. The anti-theologians use the revealed Word of God to show that there can be no revealed Word of God – or that if there could, it would remain impenetrable darkness and Mystery to our finite minds.

Nonsense Has Come

Is it any wonder that the world is grasping at straws – the straws of experientialism, mysticism, and drugs? After all, if people are told that the Bible contains insoluble mysteries, then is not a flight into mysticism to be expected? On what grounds can it be condemned? Certainly not on logical grounds or Biblical grounds, if logic is futile and the Bible unknowable. Moreover, if it cannot be condemned on logical or Biblical grounds, it cannot be condemned at all. If people are going to have a religion of the mysterious, they will not adopt Christianity: They will have a genuine mystery religion. The popularity of mysticism, drugs, and religious experience is the logical consequence of the irrationalism of the present age. There can and will be no Christian reformation – and no restoration of a free society – unless and until the irrationalism of the age is totally repudiated by Christians.

The Church Defenseless

Yet how shall they do it? The official spokesmen for Christianity have been fatally infected with irrationalism. The seminaries, which annually train thousands of men to teach millions of Christians, are the finishing schools of irrationalism, completing the job begun by the government schools and colleges. Most of the pulpits of the conservative churches (we are not speaking of the obviously apostate churches) are occupied

143

by graduates of the anti-theological schools. These products of modern anti-theological education, when asked to give a reason for the hope that is in them, can generally respond with only the intellectual analogue of a shrug – a mumble about Mystery. They have not grasped – and therefore cannot teach those for whom they are responsible – the first truth: "And you shall know the truth." Many, in fact, explicitly contradict Christ, saying that, at best, we possess only "pointers" to the truth, or something "similar" to the truth, a mere analogy. Is the impotence of the Christian church a puzzle? Is the fascination with Pentecostalism, faith healing, Eastern Orthodoxy, and Roman Catholicism – all sensate and anti-intellectual religions – among members of Christian churches an enigma? Not when one understands the pious nonsense that is purveyed in the name of God in the religious colleges and seminaries.

The Trinity Foundation

The creators of The Trinity Foundation firmly believe that theology is too important to be left to the licensed theologians – the graduates of the schools of theology. They have created The Trinity Foundation for the express purpose of teaching believers all that the Scriptures contain – not warmed over, baptized, Antichristian philosophies. Each member of the board of directors of The Trinity Foundation has signed this oath: "I believe that the Bible alone and the Bible in its entirety is the Word of God and, therefore, inerrant in the autographs. I believe that the system of truth presented in the Bible is best summarized in the *Westminster Confession of Faith*. So help me God."

The ministry of The Trinity Foundation is the presentation of the system of truth taught in Scripture as clearly and as completely as possible. We do not regard obscurity as a virtue, nor confusion as a sign of spirituality. Confusion, like all error, is sin, and teaching that confusion is all that Christians can hope for is doubly sin.

The presentation of the truth of Scripture necessarily involves the rejection of error. The Foundation has exposed and will continue to expose the irrationalism of the present age, whether its current spokesman be an existentialist philosopher or a professed Reformed theologian. We oppose anti-intellectualism, whether it be espoused by a Neo-orthodox theologian or a fundamentalist evangelist. We reject misology, whether it be on the lips of a Neo-evangelical or those of a Roman Catholic Charismatic. We repudiate agnosticism, whether it be secular or religious. To each error we bring the brilliant light of Scripture, proving all things, and holding fast to that which is true.

The Primacy of Theory

The ministry of The Trinity Foundation is not a "practical" ministry. If you are a pastor, we will not enlighten you on how to organize an ecumenical prayer meeting in your community or how to double church attendance in a year. If you are a homemaker, you will have to read elsewhere to find out how to become a total woman. If you are a businessman, we will not tell you how to develop a social conscience. The professing church is drowning in such "practical" advice.

The Trinity Foundation is unapologetically theoretical in its outlook, believing that theory without practice is dead, and that practice without theory is blind. The trouble with the professing church is not primarily in its practice, but in its theory. Churchgoers and teachers do not know, and many do not even care to know, the doctrines of Scripture. Doctrine is intellectual, and churchgoers and teachers are generally anti-intellectual. Doctrine is ivory tower philosophy, and they scorn ivory towers. The ivory tower, however, is the control tower of a civilization. It is a fundamental, theoretical mistake of the "practical" men to think that they can be merely practical, for practice is always the practice of some theory. The relationship between theory and practice is the relationship between cause and effect. If a person believes correct theory, his practice will tend to be correct. The practice of contemporary Christians is immoral because it is the practice of false theories. It is a major theoretical mistake of the "practical" men to think that they can ignore the ivory towers of the philosophers and theologians as irrelevant to their lives. Every action that "practical" men take is governed by the thinking that has occurred in some ivory tower – whether that tower be the British Museum; the Academy; a home in Basel, Switzerland; or a tent in Israel.

In Understanding Be Men

It is the first duty of the Christian to understand correct theory – correct doctrine – and thereby implement correct practice. This order – first theory, then practice – is both logical and Biblical. It is, for example, exhibited in Paul's *Epistle to the Romans,* in which he spends the first eleven chapters expounding theory and the last five discussing practice. The contemporary teachers of Christians have not only reversed the Biblical order, they have inverted the Pauline emphasis on theory and practice. The virtually complete failure of the teachers of the professing church to instruct believers in correct doctrine is the cause of the misconduct and spiritual and cultural impotence of Christians. The church's lack of power is the result of its lack of truth. The *Gospel* is the power of God, not religious experiences or personal relationships. The church has no power because it has abandoned the Gospel, the good news, for a religion of experientialism. Twentieth-first-century American churchgoers are children carried about by every wind of doctrine, not knowing what they believe, or even if they believe anything for certain.

The chief purpose of The Trinity Foundation is to counteract the irrationalism of the age and to expose the errors of the teachers of the church. Our emphasis – on the Bible as the sole source of knowledge, on the primacy of truth, on the supreme importance of correct doctrine, and on the necessity for systematic and logical thinking – is almost unique. To the extent that the church survives – and she will survive and flourish – it will be because of her increasing acceptance of these basic ideas and their logical implications.

We believe that The Trinity Foundation is filling a vacuum. We are saying that Christianity is intellectually defensible – that, in fact, it is the only intellectually defensible system of thought. We are saying that God has made the wisdom of this world – whether that wisdom be called science, religion, philosophy, or common sense – foolishness. We are appealing to all Christians who have not conceded defeat in the intellectual battle with the world to join us in our efforts to raise a standard to which all men of sound mind can repair.

The love of truth, of God's Word, has all but disappeared in our time. We are committed to and pray for a great instauration. But though we may not see this reformation in our lifetimes, we believe it is our duty to present the whole counsel of God, because Christ has commanded it. The results of our teaching are in God's hands, not ours. Whatever those results, his Word is never taught in vain, but always accomplishes the result that he intended it to accomplish. Professor Gordon H. Clark has stated our view well:

> There have been times in the history of God's people, for example, in the days of Jeremiah, when refreshing grace and widespread revival were not to be expected: The time was one of chastisement. If this twentieth century is of a similar nature, individual Christians here and there can find comfort and strength in a study of God's Word. But if God has decreed happier days for us, and if we may expect a world-shaking and genuine spiritual awakening, then it is the author's belief that a zeal for souls, however necessary, is not the sufficient condition. Have there not been devout saints in every age, numerous enough to carry on a revival? Twelve such persons are plenty. What distinguishes the arid ages from the period of

the Reformation, when nations were moved as they had not been since Paul preached in Ephesus, Corinth, and Rome, is the latter's fullness of knowledge of God's Word. To echo an early Reformation thought, when the ploughman and the garage attendant know the Bible as well as the theologian does, and know it better than some contemporary theologians, then the desired awakening shall have already occurred.

In addition to publishing books, the Foundation publishes a monthly newsletter, *The Trinity Review*. Subscriptions to *The Review* are free to U.S. addresses; please write to the address on the order form to become a subscriber. If you would like further information or would like to join us in our work, please let us know.

The Trinity Foundation is a non-profit foundation, tax exempt under section 501 (c)(3) of the Internal Revenue Code of 1954. You can help us disseminate the Word of God through your tax-deductible contributions to the Foundation.

John W. Robbins

INTELLECTUAL AMMUNITION

The Trinity Foundation is committed to bringing every philosophical and theological thought captive to Christ. The books listed below are designed to accomplish that goal. They are written with two subordinate purposes: (1) to demolish all non-Christian claims to knowledge; and (2) to build a system of truth based upon the Bible alone.

Philosophy

Ancient Philosophy
Gordon H. Clark   Trade paperback $24.95
This book covers the thousand years from the Pre-Socratics to Plotinus. It represents some of the early work of Dr. Clark – the work that made his academic reputation. It is an excellent college text.

Behaviorism and Christianity
Gordon H. Clark   Trade paperback $5.95
Behaviorism *is a critique of both secular and religious behaviorists. It includes chapters on John Watson, Edgar S. Singer, Jr., Gilbert Ryle, B. F. Skinner, and Donald MacKay. Clark's refutation of behaviorism and his argument for a Christian doctrine of man are unanswerable.*

Christ and Civilization
John W. Robbins   Trade paperback $3.95
Civilization as we know it is a result of the widespread proclamation and belief of the Gospel of justification by faith alone in the

sixteenth century. Christ foretold this result in the Sermon on the Mount: "Seek first the Kingdom of God and his righteousness, and all these things will be added to you."

This brief overview of the history of western civilization makes it clear that our cultural debt is to the Gospel, not to Greece and Rome.

Christian Philosophy   Hardback $29.95
Gordon H. Clark   Trade paperback $21.95

This book, Volume 4 in The Works of Gordon Haddon Clark, *combines three of his most important works in philosophy:* Three Types of Religious Philosophy; Religion, Reason and Revelation; *and* An Introduction to Christian Philosophy. *Together they constitute Dr. Clark's principal statement of his Christian philosophy.*

A Christian Philosophy of Education   Hardback $18.95
Gordon H. Clark   Trade paperback $12.95

The first edition of this book was published in 1946. It sparked the contemporary interest in Christian schools. In the 1970s, Dr. Clark thoroughly revised and updated it, and it is needed now more than ever. Its chapters include: The Need for a World-View; The Christian World-View; The Alternative to Christian Theism; Neutrality; Ethics; The Christian Philosophy of Education; Academic Matters; and Kindergarten to University. Three appendices are included: The Relationship of Public Education to Christianity; A Protestant World-View; and Art and the Gospel. This is Volume 10 in The Works of Gordon Haddon Clark.

A Christian View of Men and Things   Hardback $29.95
Gordon H. Clark   Trade paperback $14.95

No other book achieves what A Christian View *does: the presentation of Christianity as it applies to history, politics, ethics, science, religion, and epistemology. Dr. Clark's command of both worldly philosophy and Scripture is evident on every page, and the result is a*

breathtaking and invigorating challenge to the wisdom of this world.
This is Volume 1 *in* The Works of Gordon Haddon Clark.

Clark Speaks from the Grave
Gordon H. Clark   Trade paperback $3.95
   Dr. Clark chides some of his critics for their failure to defend Chris-
tianity competently. Clark Speaks *is a stimulating and illuminating*
discussion of the errors of contemporary apologists.

Ecclesiastical Megalomania: The Economic and Political Thought of the Roman Catholic Church
John W. Robbins   Hardback $21.95
   This detailed and thorough analysis and critique of the social teach-
ing of the Roman Church-State is the only such book available by a
Christian economist and political philosopher. The book's conclusions
reveal the Roman Church-State to be an advocate of its own brand of
faith-based fascism. Ecclesiastical Megalomania *includes the com-*
plete text of the Donation of Constantine *and Lorenzo Valla's*
exposé of the hoax.

Education, Christianity, and the State
J. Gresham Machen   Trade paperback $10.95
   Machen was one of the foremost educators, theologians, and defend-
ers of Christianity in the twentieth century. The author of several
scholarly books, Machen saw clearly that if Christianity is to survive
and flourish, a system of Christian schools must be established. This
collection of essays and speeches captures his thoughts on education
over nearly three decades.

Essays on Ethics and Politics
Gordon H. Clark   Trade paperback $10.95
   Dr. Clark's essays, written over the course of five decades, are a
major statement of Christian ethics.

Gordon H. Clark: Personal Recollections
John W. Robbins, editor   Trade paperback $6.95
  Friends of Dr. Clark have written their recollections of the man. Contributors include family members, colleagues, students, and friends such as Harold Lindsell, Carl Henry, Ronald Nash, and Anna Marie Hager.

Historiography: Secular and Religious
Gordon H. Clark   Trade paperback $13.95
  In this masterful work, Dr. Clark applies his philosophy to the writing of history, examining all the major schools of historiography.

Language and Theology
Gordon H. Clark   Trade paperback $9.95
  There were two main currents in twentieth-century philosophy – Language Philosophy and Existentialism. Both were hostile to Christianity. Dr. Clark disposes of language philosophy in this brilliant critique of Bertrand Russell, Ludwig Wittgenstein, Rudolf Carnap, A. J. Ayer, Langdon Gilkey, and many others.

Logic
Gordon H. Clark   Hardback $16.95
  Written as a textbook for Christian schools, Logic *is another unique book from Dr. Clark's pen. His presentation of the laws of thought, which must be followed if Scripture is to be understood correctly, and which are found in Scripture itself, is both clear and thorough.* Logic *is an indispensable book for the thinking Christian.*

Lord God of Truth, Concerning the Teacher
Gordon H. Clark and
Aurelius Augustine   Trade paperback $7.95
  This essay by Dr. Clark summarizes many of the most telling arguments against empiricism and defends the Biblical teaching that we know God and truth immediately. The dialogue by Augustine is a refutation of empirical language philosophy.

The Philosophy of Science and Belief in God
Gordon H. Clark   Trade paperback $8.95

In opposing the contemporary idolatry of science, Dr. Clark analyzes three major aspects of science: the problem of motion, Newtonian science, and modern theories of physics. His conclusion is that science, while it may be useful, is always false; and he demonstrates its falsity in numerous ways. Since science is always false, it can offer no alternative to the Bible and Christianity.

Religion, Reason and Revelation
Gordon H. Clark   Trade paperback $10.95

One of Dr. Clark's apologetical masterpieces, Religion, Reason and Revelation *has been praised for the clarity of its thought and language. It includes these chapters: Is Christianity a Religion? Faith and Reason; Inspiration and Language; Revelation and Morality; and God and Evil. It is must reading for all serious Christians.*

The Scripturalism of Gordon H. Clark
W. Gary Crampton   Trade paperback $9.95

Dr. Crampton has written an introduction to the philosophy of Gordon H. Clark that is helpful to both beginners and advanced students of theology. This book includes a bibliography of Dr. Clark's works.

Thales to Dewey:
A History of Philosophy   Hardback $29.95
Gordon H. Clark   Trade paperback $21.95

This is the best one-volume history of philosophy in print. This is Volume 3 *in* The Works of Gordon Haddon Clark.

Three Types of Religious Philosophy
Gordon H. Clark   Trade paperback $6.95

In this book on apologetics, Dr. Clark examines empiricism, rationalism, dogmatism, and contemporary irrationalism, which does not

153

rise to the level of philosophy. He offers an answer to the question, "How can Christianity be defended before the world?"

William James and John Dewey
Gordon H. Clark   Trade paperback $8.95
William James and John Dewey are two of the most influential philosophers America has produced. Their philosophies of Instrumentalism and Pragmatism are hostile to Christianity, and Dr. Clark demolishes their arguments.

Without A Prayer: Ayn Rand and the Close of Her System
John W. Robbins   Hardback $27.95
Ayn Rand has been a best-selling author since 1957. Without A Prayer discusses Objectivism's epistemology, theology, ethics, and politics in detail. Appendices include analyses of books by Leonard Peikoff and David Kelley, as well as several essays on Christianity and philosophy.

Theology

Against the Churches: The Trinity Review 1989-1998
John W. Robbins, editor   Oversize hardback $39.95
This is the second volume of essays from The Trinity Review, *covering its second ten years, 1989-1998. This volume, like the first, is fully indexed and is very useful in research and in the classroom. Authors include: Gordon Clark, John Robbins, Charles Hodge, J. C. Ryle, Horatius Bonar, and Robert L. Dabney.*

Against the World: The Trinity Review 1978-1988
John W. Robbins, editor   Oversize hardback $34.95
This is a clothbound collection of the essays published in The Trinity Review *from 1978 to 1988, 70 in all. It is a valuable source of information and arguments explaining and defending Christianity.*

The Atonement
Gordon H. Clark   Trade paperback $8.95

In The Atonement, *Dr. Clark discusses the covenants, the virgin birth and incarnation, federal headship and representation, the relationship between God's sovereignty and justice, and much more. He analyzes traditional views of the atonement and criticizes them in the light of Scripture alone.*

The Biblical Doctrine of Man
Gordon H. Clark   Trade paperback $6.95

Is man soul and body or soul, spirit, and body? What is the image of God? Is Adam's sin imputed to his children? Is evolution true? Are men totally depraved? What is the heart? These are some of the questions discussed and answered from Scripture in this book.

By Scripture Alone
W. Gary Crampton   Trade paperback $12.95

This is a clear and thorough explanation of the Scriptural doctrine of Scripture and a refutation of the recent Romanist attack on Scripture as the Word of God.

The Changing of the Guard
Mark W. Karlberg   Trade paperback $3.95

This essay is a critical discussion of Westminster Seminary's anti-Reformational and un-Biblical teaching on the doctrine of justification. Dr. Karlberg exposes the doctrine of justification by faith and works – not sola fide *– taught at Westminster Seminary for the past 25 years, by Professors Norman Shepherd, Richard Gaffin, John Frame, and others.*

The Church Effeminate
John W. Robbins, editor   Hardback $29.95

This is a collection of 39 essays by the best theologians of the church on the doctrine of the church: Martin Luther, John Calvin, Benjamin

Warfield, Gordon Clark, J. C. Ryle, and many more. The essays cover the structure, function, and purpose of the church.

The Clark-Van Til Controversy
Herman Hoeksema   Trade paperback $7.95
This collection of essays by the founder of the Protestant Reformed Churches – essays written at the time of the Clark-Van Til controversy in the 1940s – is one of the best commentaries on those events in print.

Commentaries on Paul's Letters   Hardback $29.95
Gordon H. Clark   Trade paperback $21.95
This is Volume 12 of The Works of Gordon Haddon Clark. *It combines his commentaries on* Colossians, Ephesians, First and Second Thessalonians, *and his essay* Logical Criticisms of Textual Criticism.

A Companion to The Current
Justification Controversy
John W. Robbins   Trade paperback $9.95
This book includes documentary source material not available in The Current Justification Controversy, *an essay tracing the origins and continuation of this controversy throughout American Presbyterian churches, and an essay on the New Perspective on Paul by Robert L. Reymond.*

Cornelius Van Til: The Man and The Myth
John W. Robbins   Trade paperback $2.45
The actual teachings of this eminent Philadelphia theologian have been obscured by the myths that surround him. This book penetrates those myths and criticizes Van Til's surprisingly unorthodox views of God and the Bible.

The Current Justification Controversy

O. Palmer Robertson   Trade paperback $9.95

From 1975 to 1982 a controversy over justification raged within Westminster Theological Seminary and the Philadelphia Presbytery of the Orthodox Presbyterian Church. As a member of the faculties of both Westminster and Covenant Seminaries during this period, O. Palmer Robertson was an important participant in this controversy. This is his account of the controversy, vital background for understanding the defection from the Gospel that is now widespread in Presbyterian churches.

The Everlasting Righteousness

Horatius Bonar   Trade paperback $8.95

Originally published in 1874, the language of Bonar's masterpiece on justification by faith alone has been updated and Americanized for easy reading and clear understanding. This is one of the best books ever written on justification.

God and Evil: The Problem Solved

Gordon H. Clark   Trade paperback $5.95

This volume is Chapter 5 of Religion, Reason and Revelation, *in which Dr. Clark presents his solution to the problem of evil.*

God-Breathed: The Divine Inspiration of the Bible

Louis Gaussen   Trade paperback $16.95

Gaussen, a nineteenth-century Swiss Reformed pastor, comments on hundreds of passages in which the Bible claims to be the Word of God. This is a massive defense of the doctrine of the plenary and verbal inspiration of Scripture.

God's Hammer: The Bible and Its Critics

Gordon H. Clark   Trade paperback $10.95

The starting point of Christianity, the doctrine on which all other doctrines depend, is "The Bible alone, and the Bible in its entirety, is

the Word of God written, and, therefore, inerrant in the autographs."
Over the centuries the opponents of Christianity, with Satanic shrewd-
ness, have concentrated their attacks on the truthfulness and complete-
ness of the Bible. In the twentieth century the attack was not so much
in the fields of history and archaeology as in philosophy. Dr. Clark's
brilliant defense of the complete truthfulness of the Bible is captured in
this collection of eleven major essays.

The Holy Spirit
Gordon H. Clark   Trade paperback $8.95
This discussion of the third person of the Trinity is both concise and
exact. Dr. Clark includes chapters on the work of the Spirit, sanctification,
and Pentecostalism. This book is part of his multi-volume systematic
theology that began appearing in print in 1985.

The Incarnation
Gordon H. Clark   Trade paperback $8.95
Who is Christ? The attack on the doctrine of the Incarnation in
the nineteenth and twentieth centuries was vigorous, but the ortho-
dox response was lame. Dr. Clark reconstructs the doctrine of the
Incarnation, building and improving upon the Chalcedonian
definition.

The Johannine Logos
Gordon H. Clark   Trade paperback $5.95
Dr. Clark analyzes the relationship between Christ, who is the
truth, and the Bible. He explains why John used the same word to
refer to both Christ and his teaching. Chapters deal with the Pro-
logue to John's Gospel; Logos and Rheemata; Truth; and Saving
Faith.

Justification by Faith Alone
Charles Hodge   Trade paperback $10.95
Charles Hodge of Princeton Seminary was the best American theo-
logian of the nineteenth century. Here, for the first time, are his two

major essays on justification in one volume. This book is essential in defending the faith.

Karl Barth's Theological Method
Gordon H. Clark   Trade paperback $18.95

Karl Barth's Theological Method *is perhaps the best critique of the Neo-orthodox theologian Karl Barth ever written. Dr. Clark discusses Barth's view of revelation, language, and Scripture, focusing on his method of writing theology, rather than presenting a comprehensive analysis of the details of Barth's theology.*

Logical Criticisms of Textual Criticism
Gordon H. Clark   Trade paperback $3.25

Dr. Clark's acute mind enables him to demonstrate the inconsistencies, assumptions, and flights of fancy that characterize the science of New Testament criticism.

Not Reformed at All
Medievalism in "Reformed" Churches
John Robbins and Sean Gerety   Trade paperback $9.95

This book is a response to and refutation of Douglas Wilson's book "Reformed" is Not Enough: Recovering the Objectivity of the Covenant. *Wilson, one of the leading figures in the Neolegalist movement in Reformed and Presbyterian circles, attacked covenant theology and proposed a "visible, photographable" covenant which one enters by ritual baptism, making one a Christian. Salvation received in this way can be lost by one's own lack of performance or by action of authorized representatives of the church. This refutation of Wilson is a defense of the Biblical Covenant of Grace.*

Predestination
Gordon H. Clark   Trade paperback $10.95

Dr. Clark thoroughly discusses one of the most controversial and pervasive doctrines of the Bible: that God is, quite literally, Almighty. Free will, the origin of evil, God's omniscience, creation, and the new birth are all presented within a Scriptural framework. The objections of those who do not believe in Almighty God are considered and refuted. This edition also contains the text of the booklet, Predestination in the Old Testament.

Sanctification
Gordon H. Clark   Trade paperback $8.95
   In this book, which is part of Dr. Clark's multi-volume systematic theology, he discusses historical theories of sanctification, the sacraments, and the Biblical doctrine of sanctification.

Study Guide to the Westminster Confession
W. Gary Crampton   Oversize paperback $10.95
   This Study Guide *can be used by individuals or classes. It contains a paragraph-by-paragraph summary of the* Westminster Confession, *and questions for the student to answer. Space for answers is provided. The* Guide *will be most beneficial when used in conjunction with Dr. Clark's* What Do Presbyterians Believe?

A Theology of the Holy Spirit
Frederick Dale Bruner   Trade paperback $16.95
   First published in 1970, this book has been hailed by reviewers as "thorough," "fair," "comprehensive," "devastating," "the most significant book on the Holy Spirit," and "scholarly." Gordon Clark described this book in his own book The Holy Spirit *as "a masterly and exceedingly well researched exposition of Pentecostalism. The documentation is superb, as is also his penetrating analysis of their non-scriptural and sometimes contradictory conclusions." Unfortunately, the book is marred by the author's sacramentarianism.*

The Trinity
Gordon H. Clark   Trade paperback $8.95
   Apart from the doctrine of Scripture, no teaching of the Bible is more fundamental than the doctrine of God. Dr. Clark's defense of the orthodox doctrine of the Trinity is a principal portion of his systematic

theology. There are chapters on the Deity of Christ; Augustine; the Incomprehensibility of God; Bavinck and Van Til; and the Holy Spirit; among others.

What Calvin Says
W. Gary Crampton   Trade paperback $10.95
This is a clear, readable, and thorough introduction to the theology of John Calvin.

What Do Presbyterians Believe?
Gordon H. Clark   Trade paperback $10.95
This classic is the best commentary on the Westminster Confession of Faith *ever written.*

What Is Saving Faith?
Gordon H. Clark   Trade paperback $12.95
This is the combined edition of Faith and Saving Faith *and* The Johannine Logos. *The views of the Roman Catholic Church, John Calvin, Thomas Manton, John Owen, Charles Hodge, and B. B. Warfield are discussed in this book. Is the object of faith a person or a proposition? Is faith more than belief? Is belief thinking with assent, as Augustine said? In a world chaotic with differing views of faith, Dr. Clark clearly explains the Biblical view of faith and saving faith.*

In The Johannine Logos, *Dr. Clark analyzes the relationship between Christ, who is the truth, and the Bible. He explains why John used the same word to refer to both Christ and his teaching. Chapters deal with the Prologue to John's Gospel;* Logos *and* Rheemata; Truth; *and* Saving Faith.

Clark's Commentaries
on the New Testament
Commentaries on Paul's Letters   Hardback $29.95
Trade paperback $21.95
(Colossians, Ephesians, First and Second Thessalonians)

First Corinthians	Trade paperback	$10.95
First John	Trade paperback	$10.95
New Heavens, New Earth		
(First and Second Peter)	Trade paperback	$10.95
The Pastoral Epistles	Hardback	$29.95
(1 and 2 Timothy and Titus)	Trade paperback	$14.95
Philippians	Trade paperback	$9.95

All of Clark's commentaries are expository, not technical, and are written for the Christian layman. His purpose is to explain the text clearly and accurately so that the Word of God will be thoroughly known by every Christian.

The Trinity Library

We will send you one copy of each of the books listed above for $500 (retail value $800), postpaid to any address in the U.S. You may also order the books you want individually on the order form on the next page. Because some of the books are in short supply, we must reserve the right to substitute others of equal or greater value in The Trinity Library. This special offer expires October 31, 2007.

Order Form

NAME _____

ADDRESS _____

_____

TELEPHONE _____

E-MAIL _____

Please:

❑ add my name to the mailing list for *The Trinity Review*. I understand that there is no charge for single copies of *The Review* sent to a U. S. address.

❑ accept my tax deductible contribution of $ _____ .

❑ send me _____ copies of *Logic*. I enclose as payment U.S. $ _____.

❑ send me the Trinity Library. I enclose U.S. $500 as full payment.

❑ send me the following books. I enclose full payment in the amount of U.S. $ _____ for them.

_____

_____

_____

_____

The Trinity Foundation
Post Office Box 68
Unicoi, Tennessee 37692
Website: http://www.trinityfoundation.org/
United States of America

Shipping: Please add $6.00 for the first book, and 50 cents for each additional book. For foreign orders, please add $1.00 for each additional book.